W9-CCB-529

DIGITAL STORYTELLING

Capturing Lives, Creating Community

Joe Lambert

DIGITAL STORYTELLING

Capturing Lives, Creating Community

Digital Diner Press
Berkeley, California, USA

Digital Diner Press
1803 Martin Luther King Jr. Way
Berkeley, CA 94709
510–548–2065 phone
510–548–1345 fax
www.storycenter.org

© 2002, 2006, 2009 Joe Lambert
All Rights Reserved
First Edition published: 2002
Second Edition: 2006
Third Edition: 2009

No part of this publication may be reproduced, stored in a retrieval system, or transmitted in any form or by any means, electronic, mechanical, photocopying, recording or otherwise without either the prior written permission of the publishers or author.

ISBN: 978-1-61623-849-0

First and Second Editions designed by Oakleaf Designs, Patrick and Eileen Milligan
Third Edition Cover Design and photo by Rob Kershaw
Copy Editing, proofing, and layout by Patrick Castrenze and Oriana Magnera
Pre-press by Helen Kershaw and John Munro, Lithocolor
Printed by Friesens

Cover Photo: *Street Tattoo* mural by Dan Galvez with assistance from Dan Fontes and Jos Sances, 1982, oils, 15x 220. Large scale portraits of various Oakland residents. San Pablo & West Grand, Oakland, CA (damaged from weathering)

To purchase a copy, or copies of this book, visit *www.storycenter.org*, e-mail *orders@ storycenter.org*, or call 510-548-2065.

All proceeds to benefit the Scholarship Fund of the Center for Digital Storytelling, a project of Life On The Water, Inc, a California non-profit corporation, 94-2660844.

Printed in Canada

Acknowledgments

O n behalf of my collaborators at the Center for Digital Storytelling, I would like to graciously thank a number of people for their contributions to the development of the *Digital Storytelling—Capturing Lives, Creating Community*.

To start with, we would like to thank the thousands of students who have shared their lives and stories with us and inspire our work. In particular, we want to thank Barbara French, Frank Gonzalez, Ernesto Ayala, Daniel Weinshenker, Monte Hallis, and Ann Jaeger for allowing us to share their stories. We have the greatest job in the world, and in every workshop we expand our circle of friends.

The first Digital Storytelling Workshop was at the American Film Institute in Los Angeles, and we want to thank Nick DiMartino, Harry Mott and Harry Marks who have been part of this bus from the very beginning.

We must recognize that this book itself has seeds in two projects. In 1996 we were given support by Apple Computer, led by our friends Ralph Rogers and Kelli Richards, to create the original Digital Storytelling Cookbook. Then in1998, the Institute for the Future, with particular support from our friends Kathi Vian and Bob Johansen, gave us support for *Digital Storytelling—The Creative Application of Digital Technology to the Ancient Art of Storytelling.*

We have a number of associates, including Amy Hill, Caleb Paull, Thenmozhi Soundararajan, and Pip Hardy/Tony Sumner who are interviewed in the book. who have been seminal in our understanding the applied use of our practice.

Over the years Digital Storytelling has evolved beyond our studios and our workshops with practices in numerous contexts. We look back to recognize the importance of our collaboration with countless organizations and individuals. Some of the names include Warren Hegg and the Digital Clubhouse Network, Glynda Hull at UC Berkeley, Ana Serrano and the Canadian Film Centre in Toronto, Daniel Meadows and the team at Capture Wales from the BBC, Helen Simondson and the Australian Centre for the Moving Imgage, Geska Helena Andersson and Kaos Pilots in Scandanavia, Jackie Sieppert and Faculty of Social

Work at the University of Calgary, Larry Johnson and the entire network of the New Media Consortium, the work of Delta Garden in Sweden, the Digital Story-Lab in Copenhagen, the developing work of Aline Gubrium and her associates at the University of Massachusetts (Amherst) to create our New England Center, Sai Ling Chan-Sew and our partners at the Community Behavioral Health in San Francisco, Sonke Gender Justice in South Africa, Downtown Aurora Visual Arts, and countless others.

The original work on this book was made possible principally as a collaboration with Emily Paulos, the Managing Director at CDS. Her support and guidance has remained vital to the ongoing process of evolving this text, and to the general development of the practice of Digital Storytelling. But with this edition, she took a principal lead on the newly written Seven Elements—now Seven Steps—and she deserves principal credit for the re-shaping of this core philosophy of our work. The 3rd Edition would not have been possible without the efforts of Helen Kershaw and John Munro at Lithocolor, Andrea Paulos, and the extraordinary commitment of our two AmeriCorps VISTAs, Patrick Castrenze for editing and Oriana Magnera for layout.

Finally, as a book of ideas, inspired by the Digital Storytelling Workshop, grew out of my collaboration with Nina Mullen and Dana Atchley. Nina Mullen spent nine years at my side developing our centers in San Francisco and Berkeley, and traveling the world teaching. As my life partner, she has been through this saga, and her support, and the support of our amazing children, Massimo and Amalina, has sustained me in this work.

Dana Atchley and I took the original trip on Next Exit twenty three years ago. His exit in 2000 was unbearably heartbreaking. His spirit sits over my left shoulder, keeping me laughing at my own self-serious perspectives. He would have enjoyed how this road trip has continued. To Dana.

Photograph by Rosalie Blakey Wardell

For Dana Atchley

Artist, Friend, Digital Storyteller

Your final exit was beyond reason.

Your vision will live on.

See you on the flipside.

Contents

Bibliography 177

Index 183

DIGITAL STORYTELLING

Capturing Lives, Creating Community

Introduction

"Third Edition." This sounds apocryphal. The fact that things come in threes has always been true for me: My parents had three children; I have had three careers; My greatest experience of loss was when my brother, my business partner Dana Atchley, and my mother all died within the same year; I have had three children, although one I have never known. I also think there are three major external trends shaping our work: global economics, the environment, and mobile technology. But before I try to weave those threads, let us cover the business of introducing this book.

This book was originally published in 2002. As I like to tell the story, it was a slow autumn, and we had too much time on our hands around the office, so we thought, why not write a book? But this reduction understates our expectations. We wanted to make a point with our work. The methods we had developed and practiced for over a decade needed to be valued. And there is nothing like the throw weight of pulverized dead trees molded into an artifact. We wanted to celebrate what we had accomplished and say, "Yo, that's right, baby, CDS wrote the book on Digital Storytelling." 5000 self-published and fitfully distributed copies have now found their way in the world, and it seems that some folks have found this project useful. Many times we have threatened to stop producing more books and move it to Kindle or a too-fat PDF (it's so much greener that way), but I feel that books are as much souvenirs as they are transmitters of information. So, thanks for picking up this curio.

What you will find here are a couple of contextual essays about the history and vision of our work, six chapters that talk about how you might make a digital story and use it for your personal or professional needs, and six chapters that discuss how digital storytelling has been taught and applied. This suggests that it is both a textbook and a teacher's guide.

We have had a few changes, with the most significant one being a rewrite of the Seven Elements of Digital Storytelling. These elements, have now been renamed to better reflect their purpose: The Seven Steps, along with our approach to the Story Circle, are at the core of our practice. As it is surprising to no one, our organization eventually grew with time, and people developed their own voice around these ideas. Thus the elements have evolved. And while there are still seven, a lucky number, the way they are approached is significantly different.

We have also rearranged our chapter on applications, touched up the appendices, and added an interview with our colleagues, Pip Hardy and Tony Sumner. But despite all of the changes throughout the book, a sense of the original conversations that took place when a group of us were wrestling with the formative issues of our practice can still be seen. I am happy to say much of what was written has held up well over the last decade.

Most of all, *Digital Storytelling, Capturing Lives, Creating Community* is a long conversation about our practice, and your entry into it is an invitation to join us in dialogue. You are the real reason we bothered to print this book, and we want to hear your stories, and about the stories you have been privileged to facilitate. You can find me at *joe@storycenter.org*, and learn much more about us at Center for Digital Storytelling's website: *www.storycenter.org*.

Slowing Down

I originally started this introduction in the summer of 2009, but I am just now finishing up with it, here at the end of the year, December, 2009. Such is publishing. In the summer, during my first version of the introduction, I was reacting to the end of General Motors. The US has been floated on cheap oil, and the barons of oil, auto, and steel shaped policy to create suburbia and every aspect of the sprawling, polluting, dysfunctional consumer society that defines the American dream. These were policies that went unchallenged by seven decades of economic and political leadership.

The American century is over. We are coming to that simple conclusion that we cannot drive the planet like a Chevy, wherever we want to go, over endless horizons. There is a dead end ahead. We had better slow down and change directions.

Here at the end of the year, the economic crisis seems a bit less like the dominant narrative. We are bottoming out, and while millions are still affected, the grand sense of cataclysm has greatly lessened.

Capitalism is resilient. Apocalypse is not now, not yet. The heat in the water is rising and we tadpoles just sort of sweat it out, not really concerned about the impending boiling point.

In the intermediate time of this writing, I traveled for the first time to China. The trip added enormous emphasis to the idea of capitalism's apparent power to create and destroy. China is a boom country. The sense of economic gravity, moving from the rustbelts of America through the long Walmart-built tunnel of money and merchandise to rest in China. We are now Chimerica. The fusion of East and West is no longer a culinary cliché, but a financial fact at levels of scale that are simply not conceivable. We are in the grand boat of progress together, one planet, and over the falls we will go.

What might this have to do with Digital Storytelling? In most of my writing and speaking over the last two years, I have suggested that all of the contemporary movements of change—the slow and local food movement, the do-it-yourself movement, the mindfulness, yoga and meditation movements, the emotional intelligence movement, appreciative inquiry, asset-based community development, holistic health, place-based education, community arts and storywork in a million permutations—are all responses to globalization. The more we share the stress and strain of a corporate monoculture based on greed and accumulation, the more we want a gentle authenticity of experience. The more we search for authenticity, the more we turn our attention away from the siren call of bland uniformity, and we search for something individuated. And the way to hear those stories is not to change channels, or surf the machine made media, but to listen to our own stories, our own hearts, and the stories of our rich, local communities.

All these trends share a commitment to listening, to stopping and paying attention, to each other, and to the world.

Slowing down.

Societies have momentum, but rupture can force change. Obama would not have been elected without the credit market collapse in 2008. But waiting for crisis to engender change is like waiting for a heart attack to discover healthy habits. We may now know better, but it is not easy to resist the speed of our lives, or the velocity of our appetites as a society. We know we should not wait until it is too late.

By bringing people together to share stories and make artifact out of transformative narratives, we are able to stop and take stock, and find ways to insert these snapshots of existence into our daily dialogues. This is why digital storytelling workshops never get old. Like all healthy practices, storytelling renews and changes everyone involved in the process.

Place, Story, and Healing

Our organization, the Center for Digital Storytelling, is at a crossroads. We have moved from being an arts practice, to a method to be shared in countless contexts, to our current emergence as a project-based organization focusing on the best ways to use the methods of our work over time in specific communities. If we had to sum up our learning, it would be that we see storywork, and our work in particular, as only valuable when it is owned as a technology of healing by a local population. It is a part of any number of useful recovery technologies in the face of the particular impact of globalized consumer capitalism on our identities, on our connections to each other, on the way we make our communities cohere, and our societies healthy. We need help. We either return to the sacred wisdom of place and make our world whole, or it appears we will perish, one-by-one in a series of new fangled illnesses, or in one vast collective disaster of an over-heated planet.

How can we do it? We can do it by listening, making stories, and marking place with narrative. This is the old way, the singing of our local wisdom, making maps of our conscious relation to nature, and making our selves better by sourcing our connection to the shared energy that makes life possible.

When we listen to our lives, and mark the world with stories, and when we relate those stories to place, we fill the world with ghosts, ghosts that invite us to take a moment to listen to their tales.

Over the last four years, through a process we described as storymapping, I have been doing a little research into the story in geography. When we learned of the Murmur project of our Canadian colleagues, we started paying attention to the vast shift in software and hardware development in the mobile phone industry, and to the growth of a popular geographic education model that has exploded with the coming of GoogleEarth, DIY GoogleMaps, and scores of geo-spatial tools. It has become possible for every crossing of longitude and latitude in the world, and every street corner, to be tagged with data, or better yet, a story.

What intrigued me about this potential was not how handy it would be to find the nearest coffee shop, or even how we might record narratives and make walking history tours around neighborhoods. Instead, what got me thinking was the idea of capturing the ghosts walking through our world.

I have direct experience with these ghosts of memory and the sacred places where they reside. In the future, quantum scientists will find that on some sub-atomic level there is a memory residue in all matter. Everything has a story, we just can't perceive it within the confines of our current tools for observation.

In shamanic contexts, the ability to hear and see the dead is considered a great privilege that is less a result of deep practice and more a gift. We are entering a time where we can leave behind meaningful and residual traces of our experiences to be found by anyone else strolling by with a multimedia device, not just for the now, but for the remainder of human history.

I believe informing this process with the values of first voice, of creating multiple narratives about places and stories that capture the meaning of a location in 1000 facets, facilitates not only the larger democratic project, but is also an excellent tool for our grand environmental recovery. Will having stories attached to fields and gardens, and stones, and homes, and bends in the river–stories rich with texts, voices, images, sounds–pulled up by our geo-smart communication devices, force us to stop and listen? We cannot know. We still may want to trade text messages and play Tetris as we stroll the grounds even more detached from our surroundings.

But it cannot hurt. The siren call of these stories could prove to be more powerful than our superficial discourse with each other, and with the entertainment these machines are throwing at us in endless streams. I have to believe that storymapping the world could be part of the process of our taking every place seriously–of treating all ground as hallowed, as sacred, as deserving remembrance, as deserving care. And by this deep connection, we can also embody these stories and heal ourselves.

The Story of CDS

Not long after CDS began, my son Massimo was born. In 2002 the first edition of this book premiered more or less simultaneously with the birth of my daughter Amalina. Watching them grow as CDS has grown has been extraordinary. For my wife, Nina, and I, the parallels in development were at times funny, and also a little bit frightening. An organization going through its terrible twos, acquiring self-awareness and independence at 8- and 10-years-old, pre-adolescence and adolescence in its teens is hard, nearly as hard as for each of us as individuals.

The CDS corpus has left the mom and pop heritage of its first decade, and has now become an international organization, actively delivering work in countless venues and fields. This introduction would be completely useless if it did not also include recognition and thanks to the community and large family we have become.

Emily Paulos took on the task of co-directing CDS in 2002. Emily responded to my "lick it, stick it" management style with a shaking head and friendly-yet-forceful encouragement, helping CDS to develop systems of management that laid the basis for this new phase of growth. In particular, her shepherding of our train-the-trainer program gave us a mechanism for deepening our work and moving us from a set of tools and methods to a multi-dimensional arts practice. As much as anyone, Emily is responsible for the publication of this book.

In 2005, Amy Hill brought her work to our organization. Her deeply held perspectives on social justice and gender equity, so exquisitely represented by the work of her Silence Speaks program, added vast new dimensions to the field of our practice. Her experience, her candor, and most importantly, her rigorous professionalism, has fundamentally changed our approach, and has been key to our ongoing success.

We met Daniel Weinshenker in 1999, and recognized his potential as a master digital storyteller. Daniel's support in the transition year of 2003-2004 led him to develop CDS Denver, which gave us a new model for national and international expansion. His primary contribution, beyond his eye-rolling dismissal of any self-serious and pompous perspectives coming out of my or any of the rest of our mouths, has been in his elegant refinement of our teaching approach. Daniel is a brilliant teacher, and he inspires us all to work harder to serve our students and create beautiful stories.

Across the Bay, we had heard of the fine work of one of our students, Andrea Spagat, who was working with youth in the area of substance abuse prevention. She was a generous teacher, and a great educator, so we put her in charge of our education strategy. Thus was born our educator workshops, which have helped us transition our conversations with K–12 education into less training, and more seminars on best practices and ideas for applying our ideas in the classroom. But the lure of community work kept pulling her back and now she is helping us to lead a large upswing of practice in public health.

To Gayle Nichols-Ali, Rob Kershaw, Stefani Sese, Michelle Spencer, Allison Myers, Jennifer LaFontaine, and our growing staff of program associates and staff around the world, we have much thanks. You continue to inspire us with your commitment and the endless directions you are taking our work. And finally to our local staff, Jennifer Nazzal, and Theresa Perez, I want to give a big heaping spoonful of affection. The hardest jobs are always the most important and the least appreciated, so thanks for sticking with it.

Listen deeply, tell stories.
— Joe Lambert
December, 2009

1 A Road Traveled

Evolution of the Digital Storytelling Practice

E very process has a genesis story—an arbitrary point in time to call...the beginning. When did digital storytelling begin? When I speak for a larger notion of digital storytelling, I always feel compelled to go back to the 1960s, and the spirit of democratization and humanism that forms both the politic and the practice of this work. When I speak for myself, my version of the story has three parts: My work in politics and theater in San Francisco, and the tale of when I met Dana Atchley, and I try to recall his walking into the construction site that was our theater in the Fall of 1986. And finally, I think of the moment it really made sense to anyone else, the first workshop that was held at the American Film Institute in 1993.

However, wherever the beginning really occurred, the important idea is that something new coalesced around this work, and that our trying to name and understand this process is still very much evolving. So climb up into the cab of our 18-wheel time machine and let's drive back on the road taken.

Story, Folk Songs, and the American Tradition of Celebrating Lives Lived

When I was a kid, my parents liked to host parties at our little house in Dallas, Texas. Over the years, lots of people showed up at our house: the local politicos and labor movement people, friends and neighbors, and sojourning activists and artists that found our home to be a small oasis of liberal friendliness in the desert of 1950s Texas conservatism. My favorite people were the folksingers.

The bardic tradition was resurrected in the name of social urgency in 20th century America. Joe Hill and the Wobblies found that by re-writing commentary to the tune of Salvation Army hymnals they could capture the lives and issues of working people as a form of social protest. Blues, always a reportage of life and living, found a broader audience, and captured new meaning in the context of a century of post-slavery African-American struggle that came center stage in post-WWII

American politics. Woody Guthrie lifted the Western ballad, traditional tunes for European folk culture adapted to the frontier experience, and told the stories of dustbowl desperation and New Deal optimism.

The McCarthy Era's cultural lesions could not completely erase the insurgence of democratic impulse in American music. And with one section of the rock and roll culture surfacing in the 1950s, the folk music scene provided a vital line of continuity between these voices of the centuries' first fifty years, and the explosive cultural renovation that marked the beginning of the second.

Digital storytelling is rooted fundamentally in the notion of a democratized culture that was the hallmark of the folk music, re-claimed folk culture, and cultural activist traditions of the 1960s.

As Greil Marcus wrote in the Winter 2001 issue of Granta, regarding the feelings inspired by the American folk music culture, "No one is just like anybody else. No one, in fact, is even who he or she was ever supposed to be. No one was supposed to step out from their fellows and stand alone to say their piece, to thrill those who stand and listen with the notion that, they too, might have a voice..."

Inherently sympathetic to human experience, the voices of these storytellers looked for ways to capture their own and others' sense of the extraordinary in the ordinary comings and goings of life. Where a mainstream culture provided glamorized and idealized lives of the movie star-perfect people living in dramatic and exotic situations, the populist artist in the folk traditions sought not just to portray, but to empower. This new folk culture spread as musicians worked to help find a guitar for each person in every living room, music hall, and outdoor gathering, and teach them eight chords, a set of licks, and set them off to record their own experience.

Most artistic disciplines became caught up in the democratization process of the era. In literature, new voices of women and people of color were strengthened in the greatly expanded notion of author and authority. In theater and dance, companies were formed to transform oral histories of common people into productions of broad impact and scope, and often involving the respondents in the production as actors, writers, and designers. In the visual arts, community muralism, youth arts, media interventions, and countless other riffs on the "Art for the People" idea came into being.

The legacy of this era informs educational, therapeutic, social service, professional, and civic processes in countless ways. The methods of capturing stories, reflecting on and analyzing how stories are told, and encouraging thoughtful insights about one's own experience all changed in the face of the social movements that shaped the public discourse during that time. On a level of profound under-standing, people who had the professional task of encouraging the learning, growth, and stability of other people, realized that the sense of significance that resulted when a person "found their voice, and made their story heard" was fun-damental to our healthy living. We can live better as celebrated contributors. And we can easily die from our perceived lack of significance to others, to our community, and to our society.

The Texan Gets Baptized in the Revolution

I found myself in San Francisco in 1976, bouncing around the debates of post-1960s revolutionary politics. One sector of that political movement was consumed with the debates surrounding race and social change. In the practice of criticism and self-criticism that was a currency of this kind of politics, I found large sectors of my Texas-white-boy identity being sheered away as part of transformative regeneration, as I moved toward creating a "new" Joe Lambert—one who was intricately aware of my own racism, sexism, subjectivity, and socioeconomically predetermined consciousness. In retrospect, while there was something naïve and a bit weird about this process of political correctness and multicultural immersion, there was also something liberating.

In his book, *The Politics of Authenticity: Liberalism, Christianity, and the New Left in America*, author Doug Rossinow, discusses how other activists emerging from the white-Southern, and more specifically, white-Texan, backgrounds in the Sixties tended their "conversions" to political rebelliousness as a transcendental moment. It wasn't that most of us had spiritual education (for myself, almost none) it was just that the languages of spiritual renewal were so prevalent in all aspects of the cultures around us, that using this language seemed to provide legitimacy to our crossing over to an outsider stance to the dominant culture. In deciding to link our perspective with the victims of American settlement and empire, and having shared some of the abundance created by that project, we felt fear and rupture. We were leaving home, both psychically, and for many like me, psychologically. But we were also being baptized into a new world of possibility, and the potential for a fluid, expansive identity that connected us to the motion of history.

San Francisco's cultural environment made it easy to cross over. I learned Chinese and hung out with Asian-American activists in Chinatown and the Nihon-machi (Japantown). I danced to salsa, soul, and disco in the Latino Mission district. I went out to organize tenants in the housing projects of the predominantly African-American Hunter's Point. My references of identity—the stories that I connected with—were becoming less about people that looked like me and shared my background, and more about people that I thought were heroically struggling to remake a world beyond the legacies of oppresion, racial mistrust, and class hierarchies. They just happened to be black, brown, red, and yellow, for the most part, and as such, I became a bit more identified with the syntax, language and story of those cultures in America.

Life and Life On The Water

From this perspective I entered the cultural field as a professional theater person, having trained in dramatic theory, literature, and writing, as well as the politics and sociology of art, at UC Berkeley. From 1983–1986, I worked for, and then directed the People's Theater Coalition (PTC), a non-profit organization that ran a theater, worked as an advocacy and networking service for almost twenty other local theaters, and for a couple of years, also ran a training academy. The wave of popular theater work in the Seventies had crested and broken on the beaches of the reality of the Reagan Eighties, and the PTC was itself in pieces as I took over.

I spent a couple of years holding on, and then re-organized my planning and development work to start a new operation in the Fall of 1986. With luck, I found three willing collaborators: Bill Talen, Ellen Sebastian, and Leonard Pitt—all successful experimentalists in various theatrical styles—to join me. We formed Life On The Water (LOH2O) in 1986, and opened our first season with Spalding Gray's *Swimming to Cambodia*.

Life On The Water had many things going for it. We emerged at a time when experimentation in theater, having belonged appropriately in marginal avant-garde, was somehow becoming mainstream. The 1980s began the United States' colonization of the "Culture of Cool." The trend to trend-hop in search of traces of authenticity meant that those on the margins suddenly had a place at the table of the national dialogue. This process was institutionalized in the socially democratic countries of the developed world, where the Avant-Garde became official culture in 1980s. However, in the States it was a hit-or-miss affair. Actors like Whoopi Goldberg, Willem Dafoe, John Malkovich, Anna Deveare Smith, and John Leguizamo, all coming from various experimental theater communities, could slip through the cracks and become Hollywood talent, while a whole host of other, extraordinarily talented performers could barely make ends meet. Careers of musical artists like Tracy Chapman, who was "Talkin' about Revolution," and scores of other artists in the rap/hip–hop movement also found mainstream acceptance right smack in the middle of it all.

Our theater featured an eclectic mix of experimental and community-based artists. One week we would have the latest of the East Village hipsters, and the next, a local Chicano Theater company. But perhaps we were best known as a home to solo performance—a quintessentially Eighties art-form. Contemporary solo theater had its roots in the performance art experiments in the 1960s visual arts communities, the community theater artists connecting with, and claiming, the folk tradition of "storytelling," and the collapse of the non-profit arts economy in the early eighties. Solo was cheap to produce. Half of the productions at LOH2O were solo works.

Life On The Water, along with our sister theater, Climate, ran a national festival of solo performance, *Solo Mio*, from 1990 to 1995. It was in this context that I met and began my collaboration with Dana Atchley.

The Colorado Spaceman Exits in San Francisco

Dana Atchley wandered into Life On The Water just before we opened in 1986. Our theater was being remodeled, and was based on a design by architect Minoru Takeyama. We were on a budget of ten cents, and a timeline of the-day-before yesterday. As such, a few days before the season opened the place still looked like a construction site. Dana stepped over a few 2 x 4's and introduced himself. At 45, he was approximately the same age as our season opener, Spalding Gray. And like Spalding, he had a mix of New England WASP carriage, with a twist of road wisdom and perspective. In retrospect, I think they both shared the baby boom pioneer role. Most of what middle-class white people in the U.S. experienced and thought about the 1960s first happened in the northeast United States in the late 1950s before it made its way over to the West Coast.

Dana had a show, or and idea of one, and wanted to know if we would be interested in collaborating. I agreed to go over and visit and have him give me a tour of his life's work. The show was called *Next Exit*, and it was exactly that: a guided tour of Dana's life. His idea was captured inside a large three ring binder, he said, and opening the binder there were four pages of storyboards that described some of the stories and the layout of his stage. I looked up at him, and then back at the binder, and then back at him again, "Okay ... uh, so what can we do?" I asked.

Dana explained that for the last twenty years he had been traveling around the country collecting roadside Americana—stories about offbeat Americans—as a sort of artistic practice. In the 1970s, his touring project was called *Roadshow*, and consisted of him singing, telling stories, and projecting slides of these oddities; touring colleges, art schools, and community centers. In the 1980s he had taken on the role of commercial video producer, working for Showtime, *Evening* Magazine and French Television, producing short "Video Postcards" in the context of licensing his content to commercial sources. Dana missed the stage, and wanted to build this show to get back into the arts after his seven-year hiatus.

Dana stayed close to our theater, assisting with some video documentation of one of our performances, and joining us at special events and openings. I explained the situation of fundraising, programming, and management of the project, just as I had to do with numerous other artists who wanted to be produced by our theater. As I left, I am sure I thought, *He's too ambitious, and he needs to develop more of a project before we can search for support. I wish him luck.* In all truthfulness, I didn't really think it would go anywhere.

The next time we met, the three-ring binder had fifty pages, up from four pages the last time we met, and he had three or four new pieces to show me that he had produced for the show. I agreed to write a few grants for the project, and somewhat as I expected, they were not funded. In the Spring of 1990, Dana said he would produce the work on his own, in his Mission District studio. I said I thought that a workshopping process would make sense, so I agreed to help with the show and to link it to our first *Solo Mio Festival*.

In September of 1990, Dana did a four-week run at his studio. At this point, the binder was full, and he had about 40 episodes organized into over an hour of performance time. The central metaphor was the campfire, with Dana entering the stage and sitting down next to a video monitor that he would "light," and would play a tape loop of a roaring campfire. Behind him was a large projected backdrop, usually a drive-in movie theater outline, inside of which the various video segments would screen. Dana would then both narrate and interact with the video segments as they advanced.

As this started, Dana was forced to rely an operator/stage hand to assist him in starting and stopping the video deck. In his first performances, this naturally led to a mechanical performance as he slowed down or sped up his narration to remain in sync with the video segments in parts of the performance. This was less than satisfactory.

But even in these early performances, Dana's design choices and approaches to the subjects of *Next Exit* encouraged many people who watched the performance to think, *"Yes, I have a story like this."* His subject matter concerned five decades of his life. He had stories of his youth and included stories about camp, elementary school crushes, learning to drive, and his father's obsession with ham radio. Additionally, he had stories of his college days and coming of age as a young artist, his mentors, his travels, and his marriage and divorce. He also had stories detailing the beginning of his days as a traveling performer/experimental artist in the 1970s, and the many colorful characters he met on the road, as well as the loneliness he felt in spending time away from his children. And finally, he had stories of his days as a professional video producer covering hundreds of thousands of miles shooting an odd assortment of American attractions.

Dana was an Ivy League–trained graphic artist, and had over a decade of work in video, but his design approach was, for the most part, transparent. He chose very approachable icons such as the road and the myth of the American highway, the campfire, the big painted skies of the American West, Americana, the family album, and home movies. He interpreted those icons through video segments that, while superbly produced, rarely called attention to their refinement. His own performance style was direct, informal, and conversational, which also tended to diminish the distance between him as performer and his audience.

Next Exit survived a couple of runs in his studio in 1990, but in 1991, with encouragement from me and others, he went back and rewrote the piece to make the performance more coherent, and to examine and re-tool the technologies he used for executing the evening. The 1991 performance run had him intertwining the themes of the evening effectively, and ending the performance on a more focused, and transcendent note. He also traded the video decks for Laser Discs that could be controlled by MIDI software on a computer, giving him increased flexibility in performance.

By 1992, the show began to travel around the Technology and Arts network of exhibitions, trade shows, and special events around California. As part of this process, Dana was introduced to the possibility of bringing his videos onto the computer through the great improvements in Apple's Quicktime technology. He met and began a long collaboration with Patrick Milligan, an interactive-authoring-design professional. Patrick adapted Dana's set backdrop design that had been accomplished with slide and video projectors, and created a computer-based interface with Macromedia's Director tool.

Computer Art had generally been associated with conceptually "cool" and experimental expression, demonstrating what the "computer" could create as much as the point of view of the artist-creator. In this context, *Next Exit* was a sharp contrast. Populist, transparent, and emotionally direct, Dana's performance spoke directly to a large section of the new media audience that still liked to hear a good story that was well told.

An Exit Called Hollywood: 1993 at the American Film Institute

One of the great ironies of Dana Atchley's personal story was that in 1980 he was approached by a producer with Lorimar Productions (the people that brought you *Dallas*) with a made-for-TV offer on his life as a traveling artist collecting treasures of Americana. Dana signed an initial agreement for a relatively small amount of money. When the movie deal fell through, for various reasons, the fine print stipulated that the character he portrayed in *Roadshow, the Ace of Space,* was no longer his. He had sold his identity, and a small part of his soul, to the devil, and as he told it, spent his 40th birthday in 1981 in the town of Nothing, Arizona. When you've seen Nothing, you've seen everything.

Thus, it confounded him a bit when he received a call in the autumn of 1992 from the American Film Institute in Los Angeles to be a featured performer at their upcoming *National Video Festival*. Dana was also asked to lead a workshop in their new Digital Media Computer Lab, having people make short, personal video-stories similar in style to the stories that he had been telling for years.

The backdrop for this event was what can only be called the Digital Tsunami of 1992 in California. The San Francisco Bay Area happened to host a little place called Silicon Valley, and as such, the engineers had been letting artists play with their toys for three decades. When the potential of desktop computing reached the frontier of multimedia, still and moving image, and text and sound, there was a thunderous explosion of activity. Just before the dot-com boom, there was the interactive media mini-boom. Money seemed to appear out of nowhere, and artists jumped ship from photography, film/video, graphic design, radio and television to try and position themselves in the "second gold rush" that they perceived was taking place before their eyes.

In San Francisco, Dana invited me to an exhibition of work at a local professional meeting, the International Interactive Communications Society. Once there, I felt the electricity coursing through the room. The 100-person capacity of the room was overflowing. I invited the group to hold their next meeting at my 200-seat theater, and 400 people showed up four weeks later. I caught the very bug that was led by collaborators in the performing arts like Mark Petrakis and Randall Packer, and saw the need for the performing arts community to be in dialogue with this sector.

When Dana, Patrick, and I arrived in Los Angeles, in February of 1993, we felt confident that we would make a good impression. Dana's performance had improved, the technology was increasingly stable, and the audience was going to be folks that could easily spread the word about this show. Of course, the idea of spending a weekend learning digital video editing intrigued me particularly, because while I had worked closely with Dana in the video production, and had seen the toolsets demonstrated, I hadn't yet put any stories together myself.

In fact, the show had a nearly disastrous beginning. Dana had made some adjustments, and the computer and the projector seemed uninterested in working together. With some last minute work by Patrick, and with me laughing on the side, *Next Exit* was performed and it was a resounding success. In the audience sat Dana's future wife and collaborator Denise Aungst. So impressed was she, that she left making up her mind to marry him.

The workshop had similar affect. The ten-or-so participants fell into their projects with a demanding intensity. The time flew by. We started with a Friday night introduction and worked throughout Saturday and Sunday, and then it was time to leave. I made a small piece about my parents wedding in Texas. And while I returned to the Bay Area, the final piece of magic appeared at the showing of the pieces at a Tuesday night salon hosted by the well-known broadcast designer and digital guru, Harry Marks.

One of the participants, Monte Hallis, a production designer in LA, had produced a story about her relationship with a young mother, Tanya, who was carrying on her own battle with AIDS while trying to organize support for other parents facing terminal illnesses. As it happened, Monte arrived late to the screening. She set an empty chair before the screen, and reported that Tanya had died just a few hours before. Soon after, her powerful and direct story was premiered. As Dana later reported, there wasn't a dry eye in the house.

Inspirations and Transformations

Dana, Patrick, and I returned two more times to Los Angeles in 1993 to lead workshops at the AFI. Each time I felt something in the process that inexplicably moved me. I had experienced drama therapy, group art exchanges, and creative writing courses that were emotionally powerful, but the process of turning story into the medium of film in such a short amount of time (three days), defied my attempts at characterization. It was "like" many things, but it was also so unlike anything I had ever seen before. The sense of transformation of the material, and the resulting sense of accomplishment, went well-beyond the familiar forms of creative activity I could reference. And even as the tools themselves frustrated me, I knew that this activity had a special power that could be shaped into a formal creative practice.

I came to understand that mixing digital photography and non-linear editing are a tremendous play space for people. They can experiment and realize the trans-formations of these familiar objects—the photos, the movies, and the artifacts—in a way that enlivens their relationship to the objects. Because this creative play is grounded in important stories the workshop participants want to tell, it can become a truly transcendent experience.

Those of us that work with story know that in conversational storytelling around tables and public gatherings, stories lead to stories lead to stories. We can watch the patterns unfold as each story transforms the conversations, the meaning, and the exchange into deeper and more intimate communication. There is so much invisible power in this simple activity that people walk away from some gatherings feeling transformed, while having little-or-no-sense of the process that brought them there.

A critical component of our success in that first year were the inspiring stories that were shown leading into the workshop experience. In 1993, these were the design examples in Dana's show. But immediately, stories like Monte Hallis' *Tanya*, for instance, became *the* example as it reflected the achievements of the two and three-day process. As our catalogue of examples grew into the hundreds, and then the thousands, we have been able to show stories on innumerable subjects and contexts when necessitated by the occasion.

As a result of the AFI experience, numerous events unfolded within the year. We had closed down the theater operations of Life On The Water, reducing the organization from nineteen people to three. I moved Life On The Water to the studio adjacent Dana Atchley's loft in the Mission and Dana and I organized what became a long-running series of informal salons called *Joe's Digital Diner*, which brought together leaders in the new media design field. Life On The Water took out a $50,000 loan to purchase six workstations and all of the necessary audio/visual equipment to offer digital storytelling classes. Then, we produced a six-week Thursday night run of *Next Exit* that was followed by six weeks of digital storytelling workshops in the Spring of 1994 and we hired my wife, Nina Mullen, as a staff member to work on this project. Life On The Water began doing business as the San Francisco Digital Media Center, and produced a calendar of classes conducted by a wide array of teachers, including the first HTML authoring class for the San Francisco community. Change happened, and the rest was history.

2 Meaning and the Memory Box

Looking back from 2020

We have a seven-year-old son, Massimo. By the year 2020, he will be 25 years old. If all goes as planned, he will be in his early-professional work-life. At about the same time, again if things go as planned, Nina and I will be looking to retire. We try to imagine this time.

A typical day at the house. Joe sits on the deck with his little Memory Box. Nina is busy gardening.

"Nina, could you help me with this thing here?"

"Joe, I'm busy trying to get my bulbs in the ground. Can't it wait?"

"Just a second, honey. I just want you to look at this."

"Oh, all right. Are you still trying to make that HC?"

"Nina, it's just a little project for the digital storytelling banquet next week. I promised I would get it done by Friday and e-mail it to the staff. Look here, I have this footage back in '02 when Massi was getting his first computer for school. I wanted to show how difficult it was to run those horrid PCs. But I can't quite figure out how to make the holographic cinema capture that Wintel machine melting right in the old piece of video."

"So why don't you call your son and ask him? He's the one who gave you the software."

"Good idea...see? You helped. Now you can go on back to your bulbs."

"Joe, you never change." *She exits. He speaks to the box in front of him.*

"Get me Massimo, you pile of crap."

A moment's pause. A voice comes over the machine. "Hello, Noorooz Masonry Design. Massimo speaking."

"Hey, Massi, got a second?"

"Yeah, Dad, what is it *this* time?"

"Just doing another little story, trying to morph in a little meltdown in an old piece of video, and it ain't working right."

"Why don't you just do it as a character animation? It's so much easier as a cartoon."

"I know, but I like those old special effects, like those stupid movies when I was younger."

"Listen, Dad, I have a presentation in half-an-hour with a client who expects me to dazzle him, and I want it to be magic. He wants our company to mason the entire facade of a war hero's museum in Novorossiysk, and I'm trying to get the dialect down for my presentation. The translation software in my box keeps slipping into Azerbaijani, and that could be a disaster. *And* the rasterizer on my VR modeling deck is barely operational. I may have to improvise the whole thing. Could I call you back?"

"Nouveau riche Russians don't know a damn thing about stonemasonry, son. You can fake it."

"Dad!"

"Okay. Okay. I'll check back. Your mom expects you to come back from Tehran for dinner this weekend, so don't forget."

"I'll be there. Bye, Dad."

Joe turns towards to the machine.

"Just you and me, babe. We're just going to have to figure it out, even if you are a sorry piece of crap. I should probably trade you in for a better model... "

The machine responds in the voice of Lauren Bacall.

"Threats aren't good for your blood pressure, honey, which is 160 /120, by the way. If you need some help, maybe you should whistle. You know how to whistle, don't you? Just put your lips together and blow."

"Damn box, just open the file."

Joe whistles.

Few things are certain about this distance into the future. The world is changing too rapidly for us to know how our myriad technology options in lifestyle support, workplace design, and civic participation will affect the youthful worker or the retiring professional. But one near certainty, in my mind, is the existence of a machine—perhaps it best be called an appliance—that will be capable of sustaining an exhaustive record of our day-to-day experiences: the Memory Box.

Our vision of the Memory Box is an amalgam of the family album, educational portfolio, home video library, scrapbook, recorder of work-related documents, media, telephone, television, scanner, audio/visual digitizer, training and application tool in every conceivable media type and metaphor of creative expression, all wrapped into one. It might even have an attitude. The Memory Box will hook into to an array of wearable and disposable input devices that will allow one to record anything at any time at resolutions far above our current television standards. And of course, it will be attached to the Internet, where it will be supplemented by a library of resources of infinite dimension.

For us old folks, the Memory Box will be the home of our family and professional archives. In retirement, we may choose to create multimedia memoirs illustrated with this collection of images and videos, make gifts for friends and family that relate our feelings for them, and also share our interests in hobbies or travel experiences with like-minded people. We might even develop political presentations to organize our neighbors to complain about the amounts of our Social Security checks. It will be how we extend all of the historic forms of interpersonal communication from the face-to-face conversation, the letter, the telephone and electronic mail. We'll grab media files to illustrate our stories as easily as we gesticulate with our hands. Whether or not people will want to listen to us will, of course, depend on how well we learn to tell a story.

For the 20-somethings of the 2020s, this appliance will provide more than hindsight. Whether he is a stonemason or an astrophysicist, my son, Massimo, will live in a world where personal media and creative expertise will be necessary for economic survival. His Memory Box will be a tool that can capture and store any experience he deems significant. Massimo will use his Memory Box to draw from any part of his historical educational/life experience portfolio, and the device will assist him in defining the meaning of those experiences and creating stories. During any number of different applications, he will have the ability to call up a wealth of references as animations, graphics, video, audio, or text.

To reach a level of economic or social security, he will have to combine the production skills of a media creative with the flexibility and shrewdness of the improvisational performer. In other words, he might have to become an excellent digital storyteller.

Digital Literacy

Telling stories about the future is an appropriate way to approach the issues of an inspirational tome. But we are not talking about tomorrow. The Memory Box is the current multimedia-capable personal computer. Thousands of communication-enhancing applications for business and pleasure are being developed each year for the computer. Millions of stories are being constructed in the digital domain every day. How many of us, if we died tomorrow, would be leaving the largest residue of our very existence on the planet etched as digital data on a hard drive?

The Memory Box exists, but we are far from becoming elegantly skilled story-tellers in these new media formats. We need a sustained effort towards digital literacy to maximize the potential of the current technologies, and to create an informed consumer who can help to shape the technologies of tomorrow. Our experience has demonstrated that project-based learning within the context of personal narrative greatly accelerates the learning process of multimedia technologies. Anything that can make the process of enhancing communications skills enjoyable and meaningful, as well as efficient, is worth your time.

Conversational Media

This is not a book about developing a screenplay for the digital feature film, or authoring the hypertext novel. While these processes are related, what we have in mind is a Memory Box filled with lots of little stories. Put together, they might represent a larger narrative, but they are really meant as singular expressions. Furthermore, they will be available for numerous presentation contexts, from a conversation across a laptop, to a 2,000-seat auditorium. We approach the story-telling part of our work as an extension of the kind of everyday storytelling that occurs around the dinner table, the bar, or the campfire.

Creating media within this conversational context also changes the way we think about media in general. We believe it is critical to sustain face-to-face communi-cation as a central means of our exchange, while the accompanying media would assist and amplify our ideas in a complementary context. Much of what we help people create would not easily stand alone as broadcast media. However, in the context of conversation, it can be extraordinarily powerful.

Thinking about conversational media shapes the way we will organize the media assets in our Memory Box. The digital images, video, music, texts, and voice will find themselves labeled according to stories and story types. These will reflect our important personal and professional relationships, moral or ethical values, critical intellectual realizations, and most valuable life experiences.

Finally, conversational media suggests that presentation of the material becomes increasingly organic, interactive, and spontaneous. Even as we are deepening our facility with creating media, we will be developing new presentational skills that emphasize improvisation.

Improvisational Identities

The idea of digital storytelling has also resonated with many people because it speaks to an undeniable need to constantly explain our identities to each other.

Identity is changing. It used to be that being German or Peruvian meant something definitive about our tastes, religion, and appearance. Our worlds were small enough that geographic or ethnic descriptors were some guarantee of expectation in sorting out ways to interact with each other. The only real way to know about someone is through story, and not one consistent story, but a number of little stories that can adjust to countless different contexts. As we improvise our ways through our multiple identities, any tool that extends our ability to communicate information about ourselves to others becomes invaluable. The digital stories that will inhabit our Memory Boxes will undoubtedly assist in this larger project of allowing us to coexist in a world of fluid identity.

Looking Backward

When I was fifteen-years-old, my father gave me a copy of a book by Edward Bellamy called *Looking Backward*. Written in the 1890s, it was a Rip Van Winkle sort of story looking 100 years into a future filled with the utopian promise of a highly technological society. It foretold, among other things, the rise of the fax machine, and also something very similar to the Internet.

My father believed in progress. Here, at the beginning of the 21st century, amid new forms of terror and counter-terrorist security measures, and with the technology boom of the 1990s quickly fading into the rear-view mirror, some of the ideas of technological progress seem more than a little foolish. My father also understood irony. You couldn't work in the labor movement in the American South and not have a full dose of ironic detachment. His message when he handed me that book was not that utopia was possible, but that we have a moral duty to imagine it. And perhaps more than that, we have a responsibility to pass along imagination from generation to generation.

The paradox of using the cutting-edge technology of digital media to encourage, in essence, a return to the ancient values of oral culture would make Dad smile.

Looking backward from 2020 to the Memory Box of today, we have a challenge to change a culture, to adapt, and to make meaning out of the efforts of our lives. Whether the promise of the Memory Box and digital storytelling becomes fact or remains a speculation is not relevant. We need to work toward its potential.

First Interlude

The Legacy of Tanya

"I never had a lot of friends, not really…The truth is that I didn't even know what one was…Growing up I was shy, and confused friendship with popularity.

Last year I met Tanya and we became the kind of friends that most friends are, acquaintances. She knew she had AIDS and would die soon, but facing death gave her more strength to live.

She had no place to leave her girls and wanted to find them a good home.

Tanya also wanted to start an organization to help parents like herself die in peace knowing their children would be loved and cared for. She also needed a real friend.

Tanya got a lot of attention the minute she told her story, as if the world had been waiting for her. I stood by and watched in amazement.

A few months later she couldn't do much on her own, and for all her efforts she felt she had only accomplished one thing … she found a real friend, and it was me…I couldn't let her dreams die with her.

The other night, Tanya told me to lay my head down next to hers. She wanted to tell me a secret … 'Monte Fay, don't forget, all we've got is where we're going…'

I couldn't believe she knew my middle name."

Tanya
—Monte Hallis
© 1993 Monte Hallis. Images and text all rights reserved.

2003 marked the 10th anniversary of our first Digital Storytelling Workshop in early February of 1993. At nearly every workshop I have taught, I have told the story of joining Dana and Patrick Milligan on the ride down to Los Angeles to participate in the workshop. Dana's show had gone well, and we gathered in a classroom on Friday night to meet the students. We went around the room of eight participants, and it seemed promising.

I remember my first impression of Monte Hallis. She was my prototype of the Los Angeles woman: blond, professional, relaxed, and self–assertive. At a place like the American Film Institute, which to an old Texas boy like me seemed like a fairly fancy place, I expected to meet folks like her. Dana was sitting at a desk with one leg folded back, checking in with folks. Monte described the story of Tanya Shaw, a mother with AIDS. Her story had inspired a number of people to take up the cause of people like Tanya. Monte wanted to do a story on her as a general profile about her inspiring work. When Monte finished her description of her story idea, I remember Dana saying, "But what does the story have to do with you?" I cannot remember her answer, but I do remember when she came back the next morning, her story had changed. And she had a fire about finishing it.

I spoke with Monte in 1998, and she told me that she stayed up all night on Saturday to finish the work. The workshop went well on Sunday with lots of great first stories. I returned to San Francisco, but Patrick and Dana stayed down for the showing on Tuesday at Harry Marks' Salon at the AFI. As they described it, the other students arrived, and movies were put on one after another. But no Monte.

She finally came in, and before her movie was shown, she put an empty chair before the large monitor. "I'm sorry I am late, but Tanya died." Monte's movie was then shown.

I would suppose, at this time, that not many stories of the thousands we have assisted have meant as much to the maker as this meant to Monte. There have been many memorial pieces. I have made several memorial stories myself. But there was something clear and something precise in the making of this tribute that continues to inspire our storytellers today.

Of the many dedications that we could offer for our work, one would certainly be to Tanya Shaw. By her example of sharing her story to organize others, even in the face of death, we are all taught a valuable lesson about dignity.

3 Stories in Our Lives

A story can be as short as explaining why you bought your first car or house, or as long as *War and Peace*. Your own desires in life, the kinds of struggles you have faced, and most importantly, the number and depth of realizations you have taken from your experience all shape your natural abilities as an effective storyteller. Translating those realizations into stories in the form of essays, memoirs, autobiographies, short stories, novels, plays, screenplays, or multimedia scripts, is mainly about time. You need time to put the raw material before you, time to learn procedures and approaches for crafting the story, and time to listen to the feedback and improve upon your efforts.

For some, conceiving an idea for a story is an easy process, while for others it is the beginning of a crisis. The issue of how we get from our conversational use of story to crafting a work that stands on its own falls more into the category of a general creative process. Why and how do we remember stories? What affects our ability to retain stories? How do we develop our own sense of voice and story? And what kinds of stories from our lives are likely to work as multimedia stories?

That Reminds Me of a Story

Cultural anthropologist Gregory Bateson was asked in the 1950s if he believed that computer-based artificial intelligence was possible. He responded that he did not know, but that he believed when you would ask a computer a yes-or-no question and it responded with "that reminds me of a story," you would be close.

Our understanding of how story is at the core of human activity has been a subject of fascination for academics and experts in the computer age. Educational and artificial intelligence theorist Roger Schank has argued in the last decade that the road to understanding human intelligence, and thus the road to artificial intelligence construction, is built on story. In Schank's 1992 book, *Tell Me a Story*, he suggests that the cyclical process of developing increasingly complex levels of stories that we apply in increasingly sophisticated ways to specific situations is one way to map the human cognitive development process. Stories are the large and small instruments of meaning and explanation that we store in our memories.

So why is it that when many of us are asked to construct a story as a formal presentation to illustrate an idea, we go blank? We informally tell stories all the time, but the conscious construction of story calls up mental blocks. Here are three possible reasons:

Overloaded Memory Bank

From the standpoint of cognitive theory, the problem is about being overwhelmed by stories that we can't process. Our minds construct a sense of memory immediately after being part of an experience or hearing a story, and unless we have a dramatic experience, or have a particular reason to constantly recite the story of the experience, it slowly diminishes in our memory. Retrieval of a given story or experience becomes more difficult the farther away we are in time from the original story or event.

In oral culture, we humans learned to retain stories as epigrams, or little tales that had a meaningful proverb at the end. The constant repetition of epigrammatic tales gave us a stock supply of references to put to appropriate use, like the hundreds of cowboy sayings I grew up with in Texas, to apply to a wide range of situations. In our current culture, many of us have not developed an epigrammatic learning equivalent to these processes.

At the same time, we are bombarded with millions of non-digestible and non-memorable story fragments every time we pick up a phone, bump into a friend, watch TV, listen to the radio, read a book or a newspaper, or browse the Web. We simply cannot process every one of these encounters and turn them into epigrams, let alone recite and retain them, and so they become a jumble of fragments that actually inhibit our ability to construct a coherent story.

Only people who develop effective filtering, indexing, and repackaging tools in their minds can manage to successfully and consistently articulate meaning that reconstructs a coherent story. We think of the skilled professionals in any given field as having developed this process for their specialty. They can tell appropriate stories—the memory of cases for a trial lawyer, for example-based on having systematized a portion of their memories. But most skilled professionals have difficulty using examples outside of their respective fields, from their personal life or non-professional experience, but those who do are often described as storytellers.

This is one of the arguments for the lifelong Memory Box as a retrieval/filtering/construction system to assist us in this process. Images, videos, sounds, and other representations of events from our life can help us to reconstruct more complete memories and therefore expand the repertoire of story that we can put to use.

The Editor

Having worked in arts education settings, we are experienced with people telling us that they have no story to tell. Along with language arts educators and
psychologists, we are aware that most of us carry around a little voice, an editor,
that tells us that what we have to say is not entertaining or substantial enough
to be heard. That editor is a composite figure of everyone in our lives who has
diminished our sense of creative ability, from family members, to teachers, to
employers, to society as a whole. We live in a culture where expert story-making
is a highly valued and rewarded craft.

Once we fall behind in developing our natural storytelling abilities to their fullest extent, it takes a much longer commitment and concentration to reclaim
those abilities. As adults, time spent in these creative endeavors is generally
considered frivolous and marginal by our society, and so few pursue it. Those
of us who have assisted people in trying to reclaim their voice know that it
requires a tremendous sensitivity to successfully bring people to a point where
they trust that the stories they do tell are vital, emotionally powerful, and
unique. Were it not that we as human beings have a deep intuitive sense of the
power of story, it's a wonder that we have a popular storytelling tradition at all.

The Good Consumer Habit

Our awareness of the residual impact of mass media has grown tremendously
over the past thirty years. Media literacy experts have thoroughly documented
that a prolonged exposure to mass media messages over time disintegrates our
critical intelligence. The process is, in part, the effect of the over-stimulation we
already mentioned. Yet, beyond the fact that we are immersed in too much TV
and other media forms, it is the style in which these media, particularly advertising, present themselves that actually affects our sense of ourselves as storytellers. If I can get more attention for the kind of shoes I wear or the style of
my hair at one-tenth the conscious effort of explaining what the heck is wrong
or right about my life in a way that moves you, why not take the simpler route
instead? Status and recognition, in our consumer culture, is an off-the-rack item.

Finding Your Story

For all of these reasons and quite a few others, a person's initial efforts at story-making can be frustrating. We have worked with several high-powered communicators who froze up like a deer in the headlights when it came time for them to construct an emotionally-compelling personal tale.

The starting point for overcoming a creative block is to start with a small idea. It is a natural tendency to want to make a novel or screenplay out of a portion of our life experiences, and to think in terms of getting all the details. But it is exactly that kind of scale that disables our memory. Our emphasis on using photographic imagery in our digital storytelling workshops facilitates the process of taking a potential story, picture-by-picture. Pedro Meyer, in creating his breathtakingly compelling *I Photograph to Remember* CD-ROM, recorded a narrative by simply setting up a tape recorder in his living room. He asked his publisher, Bob Stein, to sit beside him as he recorded his voice while he described each photograph to Bob. That was it. One take and it became the voice-over that was used for the CD-ROM. This process may work for your project.

Perhaps your project does not originate with visual material on hand. Take a look at our example interview questions in the next section for various kinds of short personal stories. Have someone interview you, then transcribe the words and see what they tell you about the story you are trying to conceive.

As you are putting together your raw material for your story, you are also working to build your narrative voice. Everyone has a unique style of expressing him or herself that can jump off the page or resonate in a storytelling presentation. Realizing your voice, and making it as rich and textured as you are as a person, takes time and practice.

The process of moving from a journalistic, technical, or official voice towards a more organic and natural voice is often difficult. It is as if we are trying to merge the two different parts of our brains: the analytical and the emotive. Most of us can't switch back and forth without getting at least slightly confused. The official voice is the voice of our expository writing class, our essays and term papers, or our formal memos and letters to our professional colleagues. We have been taught that this voice carries dispassionate authority, useful perhaps in avoiding misunderstandings, but absolutely deadly as a story.

Getting feedback also helps us identify our narrative voice. Reading material aloud to someone who we know well, and asking him or her to identify which part is true to our voice is a useful practice. Of course, crafting a narrative voice by moving away from clichés and redundancy requires pulling out the thesaurus to substitute common verbs and adjectives. But in the end, take your time and let the ideas and meanings sink in before you edit. If something feels overwhelmingly right, don't polish it too much. We have had lots of scripts that started out fresh and authentic, but by the time the authors and collaborators got through with it, it was filled with succinct and gorgeous-yet-characterless prose.

Interviewing

The following series of question sets for the "Interview" or "Self-Interview" process can assist in the development of different kinds of stories, but it is not meant to supplant a more direct scripting process if that is how you are accustomed to working. However, almost all of us can gain from having source material that appears from a less self–conscious response to a set of directed questions.

In recording your responses, you may find that you have sufficient material to make your voice-over. Cutting and rearranging your responses using digital audio editing software may be all that is required. If you take this route, keep in mind that you must take steps to ensure a good-quality recording.

Interviewing Techniques

You may find it easier to respond to these questions directly into a microphone in the privacy of your own home or office as opposed to a workshop space. If the prospect of talking to a recording device is off-putting (and it may be more likely to increase your self-consciousness than relax you), have someone interview you. This can be a friend, a spouse, relative, or co-worker. This process can be both fun and revealing, but requires that the interviewer commit to a few common-sense ideas.

Guidelines for the Interviewer

1) Study the questions so that you are not reading from the page, and feel free to ad lib. Being able to sustain eye contact assists the interviewee in relaxing and responding in a natural way.

2) Allow the interviewee to complete his or her thoughts. Unlike a radio or TV interviewer that is concerned with "dead air" in the conversation, give the interviewee all the time desired to think through and restate something that is a bit difficult to articulate. Interruptions can cause people to lose their train of thought or become self-aware and steer away from important, but perhaps emotionally difficult information. Let the interviewee tell you when he or she has finished a question before moving on to the next.

3) When appropriate, use your own intuition when asking questions to get more detailed responses. Often, a person's initial thoughts about a question only retrieves a broad outline of a memory. Feel free to request specifics or details that would clarify or expand upon a general response.

4) If the story is about information that is specifically painful or traumatic in the person's life, carefully assess how far you will allow the respondent to delve into these memories. In many situations where the interviewer is not a spouse or a loved one, you may cross into territory that is much better approached in a therapeutic environment with experienced guides or professionally trained advisors. We have come perilously close in interviews to taking people into an emotional state from which they cannot return at the session. This is embarrassing for the respondent, and an emotionally inconsiderate act on the part of the interviewer, as the interviewee may not have the therapeutic support to cope with these issues in the hours and days after the interview. Don't feel you need to hunt for emotionally charged material to make the interview effective. If it comes naturally and comfortably, so be it.

Finally, along with ensuring privacy in the interview, make sure everyone is comfortable: comfortable chairs, water at hand, and the microphone positioned so as not to disrupt ease of movement. (A lavaliere, or pin-on microphone, is the best).

Kinds of Personal Stories

There are all kinds of stories in our lives that we can develop into multimedia pieces. Here are a few sets of example questions for some of these stories. Adapting any of the question sets by integrating the existing sets, or developing a separate set, is encouraged.

The Story About Someone Important

Character Stories

How we love, are inspired by, want to recognize, and find meaning in our relationships are all aspects of our lives that are deeply important to us. Perhaps the majority of the stories created in our workshops are about a relationship, and in the best stories they tell us more about ourselves than the details of our own life story.

Memorial Stories

Honoring and remembering people who have passed is an essential part of the grieving process. These stories are often the most difficult and painful to produce, but the results can be the most powerful.

– What is, or had been, your relationship to this person?
– How would you describe this person (physical appearance, character, etc.)?
– Is there an event/incident that best captures their character?
– What about the person do/did you most enjoy?
– What about the person drives you crazy?
– What lesson did the person give to you that you feel is most important?
– If you had something to say to the person but they never had a chance to hear you say it, what would it be?

The Story About an Event in My Life

Adventure Stories

One of the reasons we travel is to break away from the normalcy of our lives and create new vivid memories. All of us who travel know that the experience is usually an invitation to challenge ourselves, to change our perspective about our lives, and to reassess meaning. We often return from these experiences with personal realizations, and the process of recounting our travel stories is as much about sharing those realizations as sharing the sense of beauty or interest in the place visited.

Strangely enough, while almost everyone tells good travel stories, it is often difficult to make an effective multimedia piece from these stories. We rarely think about constructing a story with our photographs or videos in advance of a trip. And we do not want to take ourselves out of the most exhilarating moments by taking out a camera and recording. Before your next trip, think about creating a story outline based on an idea prior to your visit, as well as what sorts of images, video, or sounds would be useful to establish the story.

Accomplishment Stories

Accomplishment stories are about achieving a goal, like graduating from school, landing a major contract, or being on the winning team in a sporting event. These stories easily fit into the desire–struggle–realization structure of a classic story. They also tend to be documented, so you might find it easy to construct a multimedia story. Televised sporting events have taken up the accomplishment story as a staple, and it might be helpful for you to carefully examine an "Olympic moment" to see how they balance the acts of establishing information, interviews, and voice-over.

– What was the event (time, place, incident, or series of incidents)?
– What was your relationship to the event?
– With whom did you experience this event?
– Was there a defining moment in the event?
– How did you feel during this event (fear, exhilaration, sharpened awareness, joy...)?
– What did the event teach you?
– How did this event change your life?

The Story About a Place in My Life

Up until this century, 90% of the world's population died within a ten-mile radius of the home where they were born and raised. While this now might be difficult for us to imagine, our sense of place is still the basis of many profound stories. One of the earliest interactive storytelling websites, *1,000 Rooms*, a German-based project, invited people to submit a single image of a room in their home and tell a story about their relationship with it. Hundreds of people responded with their own intimate stories. You may have a story about your current home, an ancestral home, a town, a park, a mountain or forest you love, a restaurant, store, or gathering place. Your insights into place give us insight about your sense of values and connection to community.

- How would you describe the place?
- With whom did you share this place?
- What general experiences do you relate to this place?
- Was there a defining experience at the place?
- What lessons about yourself do you draw from your relationship to this place?
- If you have returned to this place, how has it changed?

The Story About What I Do

For many people with professional careers, a life story is shaped by their job. Author and oral historian, Studs Terkel, collected a series of interviews in his book, *Working*, to demonstrate that we all have unique ways of perceiving and valuing what we do. And while jobs help to give some people a sense of identity, people also refer to their hobbies or social-commitments when thinking about who they are.

A good story often comes from looking at the familiar in a new way and with a new meaning. The details of the tasks, the culture of the characters that inhabit our workplace, or our spiritual or philosophical relationship to our work or avocation can lead us into many stories.

- What is your profession or ongoing interest?
- What experiences, interests, and/or knowledge in your previous life prepared you for this activity?
- Was there an initial event that most affected your decision to pursue this interest?
- Who influenced or assisted you in shaping your career, interest, or skill in this area?
- How has your profession or interest affected your life as a whole (family, friends, where you live)?
- What has been the highlight of your vocation?

Other Personal Stories

Recovery Stories

Sharing the experience of overcoming a great challenge in life is a fundamental archetype in human story making. If you can transmit the range of experience from descent, to crisis, to realization, then you can always move an audience.

Love Stories

Romance, partnership, familial or fraternal love all naturally lend themselves to the desire-struggle-realization formula. We all want to know how someone met their partner, what it was like when the baby was born, or what our relationship is with our siblings and parents. We constantly test other people's experiences in these fundamental relationships to affirm our own. These are also stories that tend to have plenty of existing documentation.

Discovery Stories

The process of learning is a rich field to mine for stories. The detective in us gets great pleasure in illustrating how we uncovered the facts to get at a truth, whether it is in fixing a broken bicycle or developing a new product.

As you decide what story would best serve your needs, keep in mind that these categories are in no way sacrosanct, and they intersect in a number of ways. It is also probable that you will come up with your own additional categories or other ways of dissecting the stories in your mind.

Don't Just Sit There...

One of the hardest, but most important thing to do is get started. Because many of these stories ask us to reveal things about ourselves that make us feel vulnerable, putting together a story can be a procrastinator's paradise. Just get up, start answering questions on a tape recorder, write things down, gather up the photos, review your videos, and bounce your ideas off of your friends and family.

Life is full of stories, but you may not have a lifetime to capture them as movies, so, go for it!

4 Seven Steps Of Digital Storytelling

During the first few years of our workshops, we would discuss with participants what made a story a digital story, and what made a digital story a good digital story. We came up with seven elements that outlined the fundamentals of digital storytelling and discovered that formally presenting them at the beginning of workshops greatly improved the process and the stories told.

Our emphasis over the years has been to help storytellers find the story they want or need to tell, and then help them clearly define that story in the form of solidly written script. For many storytellers, this process of clarification has proven to be a transformative experience, and for us, a truly rewarding journey. We now look forward to further refining this process and evolving the genre. And as we hold onto our original commitment to help storytellers sculpt a focused piece of personal writing, we will discuss what makes a story a digital story, and what makes a digital story a good digital story.

To that end, this rewrite of the elements reflects where we stand in this journey. It is not only a renaming and reordering of the elements, but a complete rethinking of our approach to digital storytelling. And because we view the storytelling process as a journey, we feel that framing our approach around the metaphor of "Steps," rather than "Elements," will more practically guide storytellers along the path of creating a meaningful digital story.

We want stories. We love stories. Stories keep us alive. Stories that come from a place of deep insight and with a knowing wink to their audience, and stories that tease us into examining our own feelings and beliefs, and stories that guide us on our own path. But most importantly, stories told as stories.

What's new in this rewrite is the idea that we are helping our storytellers fully visualize their story as a finished piece before they begin to write their script. This means that during our group process called the Story Circle, which is discussed at length later in the book, we want to help each storyteller not only find and clarify the story being told, but also check in with them about how they feel about it, identify the moment of change in their story, then use that to help them think through how the audience will see and hear their story in the form of a digital story. And finally, after the Story Circle is completed, and the storyteller has had some time alone with his or her thoughts, they can then let all of these considerations inform them as they sit down to write.

Step 1: Owning Your Insights

We want to help storytellers find and clarify what their stories are about. We often start with the question: "What's the story you want to tell?" and then as a follow-up, "What do you think your story means?" We want to hear not just what the story is about in the obvious sense: "It's about my mom, my vacation, my first real job…" But what it's really about: the storyteller, as the person who lived through the story. And what it's about between the lines. "This story is about my toaster…but really it's about losing my mom to cancer when I was five … but it's really about how that experience taught me that I am given chances to learn to trust again, over and over."

Finding and clarifying what a story is really about isn't easy. It's a journey in which a storyteller's insight or wisdom can evolve, even revealing an unexpected outcome. Helping storytellers find and own their deepest insights is the part of the journey we enjoy the most. This process can take time to unfold through check-ins and downtime during the duration of a multi-day workshop. Other questions that we ask to help storytellers are simple to ask, but can be difficult to answer: "Why this story? Why now? What makes it today's version of the story? What makes it your version of the story? Who's it for? Who's it to? How does this story show who you are? How does this story show why you are who you are?"

Finding and clarifying stories helps people to understand the context of their lives. This process of self-reflection helps move from an awareness of "I am" to a deeper awareness of "I have been … I am becoming … I am … and I will be…." As life proceeds and is reflected upon, changes can be better understood, and stories have the chance to ripen. Events from the past that may confuse a storyteller hold dormant insights that can be better understood through the realization of self-narratives. And this can happen over the course of years, or from one day to the next. This can even happen in a single moment through the act of hearing another's story of insight, and it can bring those dormant meanings to light, elucidating layers of meaning.

Our Denver Office Director, Daniel Weinshenker, borrows an aphorism from John Gardner when he facilitates storytelling workshops. All stories, they both agree, can really be boiled down to one of two types: 1) "A stranger came to town…"

or 2) "We went on a vacation." In other words, change came to you or you went towards change. These stories, in essence, fall into the widely used archetype of the symbolic journey, the journey of self-understanding. And while stories oftentimes have a journey built into them, it is important to recognize that that journey occurs for both the storyteller and the audience alike.

When we hear stories, we listen for answers that we can relate to our own lives. Honoring self-narratives through creative expression with an audience in mind, even an audience of one, offers the opportunity to not only record and string together your insights, but change how others think and feel. The way you tell a story depends on the audience. What you are trying to say, and how you say it, depends on who is listening, what they already know and don't know, and what you want them to know. What may be a story intended solely for you may end up being a story that changes someone else's thoughts or feelings. And conversely, what may be a story for someone else may end up changing the way you think or feel.

In traditional storytelling, it is commonly understood that the purpose of a story is to teach a lesson or moral. For example, if you wanted to teach a lesson to a group of children about the dangers of fire, you would tell them a story relating to fire, maybe an encounter you had in the past, so that they could better understand the danger. However, artificial intelligence theorist Roger Schank tells us that through storytelling it is in fact the teller, rather than the listener, who seeks to learn from the story told. And through the teller's repeated sharing of their story, listeners ask questions, make comments, and tell their own stories in response, which then provide the missing pieces to help the teller find a deeper meaning in their own story. This process allows the storyteller to own a more complete version of their story and move on.

But what if the story you're trying to tell isn't really yours? What if it's not about "my" anything—"my job, my mom, or my vacation." And instead, it's about "ours?" "Our life together, our divorce?" Or what if it's about "theirs?" "Their community center, their after-school program?" What then? What questions do we ask these storytellers to guide them on their journey? Reread those questions that we ask about clarifying the story—those questions that are simple to ask and hard to answer—and what do you think? We ask them all. Yes, all. In particular, we listen for the answers to these three questions: What makes it your version of the story? How does this story show who you are? And how does this story show why you are who you are? Here's Esperanza's journey of how she found and clarified the story she wanted and needed to tell:

Esperanza has decided to make a story about her non-profit, Familias Unidas, a community organization assisting low-income Latino families with negotiating the social service systems.

From the organizational brochure, and from all the grant proposals she has writ-ten, she has a great deal of information about why her organization exists and why it deserves continued community support. She also has ten years of photo-graphs from her work with community members, special events, staff members, and the several times the organization has been recognized with awards.

But as she thinks about the purpose of her story, she realizes that the organiza-tion's mission statement fails to capture the emotional essence of what they truly do, or why she's even a part of it. If the digital story is going to be present-ed to their supporters at the Christmas fundraiser, and then be placed on the website, it needs to move people and not just present a list of activities, goals, and objectives.

Esperanza decides to create a portrait of the Sanchez family, one of the fami-lies Familias Unidas has worked with. When she goes to meet with them, they express interest, but as they talk about the role of Familias Unidas in their lives, Esperanza realizes their story only touches on one or two of the six programs the organization offers. She realizes that she needs several families to capture a broad enough view about the organization in order to connect with the different stakeholders in her communities of support. "This is so much work," she thinks, "and this will never get done."

She is the director of the program, and as it is, she barely has time to work on the project. That night, she speaks with her partner, Carolina, who laughs about how Esperanza is always getting overwhelmed. "This is just like how you started the whole thing, fresh out of college," Carolina says. "You were just full of ideals. You started helping a few of your cousin's friends get some paperwork turned in for the local clinic, and the next thing I know, you were helping everyone in the barrio. You hardly slept then."

Esperanza remembered these times, how passionate she felt, and how her pas-sion inspired others to take up this work and to give donations to support it. "Maybe that's the story," she says aloud, "not just what we do, but why we do it, why I do it, and how caring starts with just one person."

She calls her cousin and asks if he would be willing to tell the story of those first projects. He says he would be honored. She starts writing, and the words flow. From this beginning story, she connects the Sanchez family's experience to show how the program became legitimized, and she finishes with a reflection on her own growth and the gifts that this work has given her.

At midnight, she closes her laptop. Esperanza sees the movie playing in her head. "I know just the images to use."

Step 2: Owning Your Emotions

As we help storytellers find and clarify what their stories are about and ask them to consider the meaning contained within their stories, we also want to help them become aware of the emotional resonance of their story. By identifying the emotions in the story, they can then decide which emotions they would like to include in their story and how they would like to convey them to their audience.

To help storytellers identify the emotions in their story, we ask a series of questions regarding their process: "As you shared your story, or story idea, what emotions did you experience? Can you identify at what points in sharing your story you felt certain emotions? If you experienced more than one emotion, were they contrasting?" And as the storyteller gains awareness of their emotional connection to the story, they can begin to think about how others might connect on an emotional level. To help storytellers decide how to convey emotional content, we ask a second set of questions: "Which emotions will best help the audience understand the journey contained within your story? Is there an overall tone that captures a central theme? Can you convey your emotions without directly using "feeling" words or relying on clichés to describe them? For example, how can you imply the idea of happiness without saying, 'I felt happy?'"

When we reflect on the emotions within in our stories, we realize that they can be complex, and with this realization we oftentimes discover deeper layers of a story's meaning. For example, stories of wedding celebrations can also be about overcoming loneliness and facing new struggles in forging lasting partnerships. Joyous births can also be about working through the fear of shouldering new responsibility. Restful vacations can also be about recognizing the stress that shapes our daily lives. Grieving the loss of a loved one can also be about appreciating the wisdom that they have imparted. Thus having an awareness of the contrasting and complex nature of a story's emotional content will not only help get us in touch with the core of the story's meaning, but also determine which emotions to include, and in what sequence to present them to help the audience understand the story.

Taking ownership of the emotions contained within a story will also help the audience connect on a deeper level. But the inclusion of emotions doesn't mean that your audience will meaningfully connect to it, so emotion alone is not the goal. When we, as an audience, hear a story that has an exaggerated tug to emotion, we read it as dishonesty. Conversely, if it seems devoid of emotion, without a hint of struggle or conflict, then we don't believe it either.

So when a storyteller wants the audience to pause long enough to listen, to listen deeply and trust them as a storyteller, they have to convey a sense of awareness and ownership of the emotions contained with their story. We want to help the storytellers be as aware of their emotions as they can be, and demonstrate to the audience that they believe in what they are saying, and are "in" their story. Unless the storyteller trusts that the audience will connect with the underlying issues of their story, they may not be fully honest with themselves or the audience.

Most audiences know that if the storyteller chooses to leave out information and describes details through inference instead of evidence, then there must be a good reason. But they can also tell the difference between being reticent and indirect, and being purposely superficial. The storyteller may or may not want to disclose intimate details, but it is beneficial for them to demonstrate a respect for their audience.

In story work, as a storyteller reflects on their sense of what the story is about and becomes aware of its emotional content, they must also choose the just-so voice that suits it. And rather than using language constructed for a society that can be judgmental and threatening, the storyteller instead peels back the protective layers and finds the voice that conveys their emotional honesty, as if speaking to a trusted friend.

Within every community, and within every shared experience, there are many different ideas of what it means to disclose information. Therefore, knowing your intended audience can shape the emotional content of your story. The degree of emotional content is also culturally specific, as storytellers are familiar with the codes and clues within their own communities. When a storyteller trusts that they are listening deeply to their own heart and imagines the thoughtful appreciation of a specific audience, they will share what is appropriate to share.

People are rarely presented with opportunities for deep, connected listening, and if they are presented with them, they often don't take the opportunity to listen with a depth that matches that of the speaker's. Therefore, our practice is predicated on providing a safe space for telling and listening to emotionally honest stories. Stories that emerge in this sacred space of deep listening can source our emotional core, and can surprise both the teller and the listener. Storytellers in our workshops often choose to address difficult issues—to wink at, stare, and sometimes engage, the demons inside. When you visit the *storycenter.org* website and view the digital stories we have chosen to share, you will see that they are diverse in theme but consistent in their emotional honesty. To paraphrase Boston-based storyteller, the late Brother Blue, the stories feel like they are traveling the shortest distance from the heart of the storyteller to the viewer's own heart.

Step 3: Finding The Moment

Finding and clarifying the insight and emotions of the story can be the most challenging and rewarding part of the storytelling process. As the storyteller becomes clear about the meaning of their story, we want to help them tell their story as a story by identifying a single moment that they can use to illustrate their insight. To help storytellers find this moment, we ask a series of questions: "What was the moment when things changed? Were you aware of it at the time? If not, what was the moment you became aware that things had changed? Is there more than one possible moment to choose from? If so, do they convey different meanings? Which most accurately conveys the meaning in your story? Can you describe the moment in detail?" Once this moment of change is identified, we help storytellers determine how it will be used to shape the story.

Our lives comprise an infinite number of moments, and some of those moments are loaded with more meaning than others. The moment of change might be the most memorable or dramatic moment, or it may have occurred without the storyteller even noticing it at the time or grasping its significance in their life. Whether the storyteller became aware of it at the time or in reflection, we want to help them find the moment of change that best represents the insight that they wish to convey. And depending on the story, they may choose from any number of moments as an entry point into their insight. For a story about trust, for example, a storyteller might choose the moment that he or she lost trust in a relationship, or regained it, or recognized its importance. Or there may be a single, obvious moment of change. For a story about a loved one's death, for example, it may be when the storyteller's phone rang and they got the news.

Reflecting on your personal insights and emotions allows you to find the moments of change that have occurred in your life. As mentioned in above discussions, audiences like to hear about change because they're looking for answers about change in their own lives. However, rather than listening to someone share their wisdom and insights with us through a report or an essay on the morals or lessons learned, we prefer when it is told to us as a story.

Compelling stories reproduce the insight and experience of the storyteller while prompting the audience to ask questions about their own experiences and look for larger truths. Compelling storytellers construct scenes to show how change happened, how they dealt with it, what they were like before the change, and what they are like after. A storyteller sharing their insight within a story says to the audience, in essence: This is what has happened and this is what I have learned. By building a scene around the moment of change, the storyteller is "showing," rather than "telling."

"Showing" through scene is part of the pleasure for the audience as they are drawn into the moment of change and actively construct their own interpretations. If you can paint the audience a portrait of both you, and your experience of the moment of change, then you are creating a scene. As you recall the moment of change, ask yourself these questions: What do you see? What do you hear? What's being said? What are your thoughts? What are your feelings? What is the context behind your feelings? Have you been in this situation before or since? Have you been in these surroundings, or had these thoughts or feelings before or since? When? Is that part of this story?

How much of a scene you build around the moment of change, how you integrate that scene into the story, and the total number of scenes depends on how much information the audience needs to know in order to understand. What happened before that moment, what happened after? Does the audience need more or less information? What are the key details that will help the audience appreciate the moment of change? Over the course of a three to five minute piece, a digital story can consist of a single scene, or it can consist of several. Because the format is relatively short, it's important to select your scenes with care and establish them concretely to ensure that they are contributing to the overall piece.

As the audience, we uncover meaning in the way the storyteller has shaped their story. The events of the story lead us to conclusions but don't constrict our own discovery, and the moment of change and the scenes built around it lead the audience to a river of understanding. However, they are the ones who have to jump in. And in this way they become participants in the narrative—to make that jump, to fill that void.

Step 4: Seeing Your Story

Finding the moment of change in your story and describing it within a scene is the starting point to telling the story as a story. However, because we help storytellers share their stories in the form of a digital story, we also want to look at how the use of visuals and sound bring things to life for the audience. There are many choices that come along with designing how the audience will "see" and "hear" the digital story. Let's begin with visuals. We discuss visual choices early in the story conception process so that storytellers consider how the use of images will shape their story. In order to "see" their story, we help storytellers describe the images that come to mind, understand what those images convey, find or create those images, and then determine how best to use them to convey their intended meaning.

As part of this process of creating a visual narrative, we ask storytellers: "What images come to mind when recalling the moment of change in the story? What images come to mind for other parts of the story?" At this point in the process, we want storytellers to simply call these images to mind, whatever they are, without being concerned about whether or not they exist as actual photos. Next, we want storytellers to explore the meaning that these images convey, and so we ask them: "Why this image? What is it conveying to you? Is the meaning explicit or implicit? Does it have more than one meaning? If so, can you describe the multiple meanings?" Once the storyteller is clear about the meaning they want to convey with their visuals, we help them decide how they will find or create these images, and how they will use them. We ask: "Do you already have these images or will you need to find or create them? How could you use the images that you already have to convey your meaning?"

In her first digital storytelling workshop, designer and filmmaker Lina Hoshino decided to tell her mother's story about the evolution of her name into Chinese and Japanese as a result of the Japanese Occupation and then the Chinese Civil War in Taiwan. At one point in her digital story, Lina shows the Nationalist Party leader, Chiang Kai-shek, in a series of images as she discusses the history. But rather than simply showing the entire formal portrait that she found in the public domain (as part of the F.D. Roosevelt Library), she chose to present the image as a series of crops and a pan.

Figure 1

Figure 2

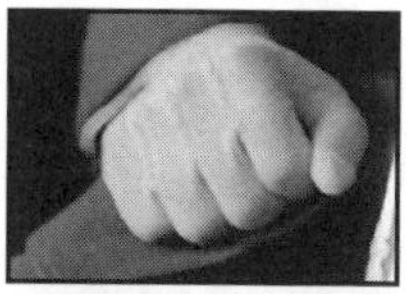

Figure 3

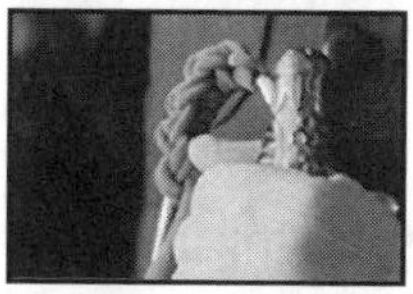

Figure 4

Figure 5

Figure 6

The original image that she found (*Figure 1*) shows the stately dictator seated with a sword in one hand and a prominently placed medal on his uniform. Lina dissects the full portrait into three cropped details that feature the medal (*Figure 2*), the resting fist (*Figure 3*), and the other hand holding the decorated hilt of the sword (*Figure 4*). After these three images, she then shows the portrait at shoulder height (*Figure 5*) and then slowly pans in and slightly to the left ending on the final frame (*Figure 6*).

Compositionally, the shots move from the medal in the left third, to the fist in the center, to the hilt/hand in the right third. The next shot, the cropped portrait of Chiang, remains in the right third of the frame. Dynamic motion across the frame is created with these detailed stills. In contrast, the slow pan returns our eyes towards the left side of the frame as we are carried along the gaze of the subject. Chiang's Kuomintang army came to Lina's mother's home island of Taiwan with imperial will. Lina amplifies this through her cropping of the image to the focus on the visual representations of power—details of the medal, gloved fist, martial hilt, and gaze of the leader.

When thinking about creating a digital story, many storytellers who are new to the form will simply envision an image that mirrors each of the different points throughout their entire narrative. These types of literal or direct images that are used to illustrate a story are called explicit imagery. Explicit imagery is useful for conveying the necessary details of your story or helping to set the scene for your audience. For example, when a storyteller says, "This is the house where I grew up" and shows a photo of a house, the audience understands that this is literally "the house." By intentionally choosing to show the house, the storyteller is also letting us know that it is important for us to see this house in order to understand the details of their story. When considering which images to use and how to use them, we want to help storytellers be clear about the important details that would not be understood or appreciated without the use of explicit imagery. To do this, we ask: "Would the audience be able to understand the story's meaning without this image?"

However, not all aspects of a story's meaning are best conveyed through the use of explicit imagery. When considering an image, a storyteller can ask: "Is this image conveying another layer of meaning?" If so, then the image has an implicit use. Implicit imagery is useful for implying or representing another meaning beyond an image's explicit or literal meaning. Two common techniques for a storyteller to convey their meaning through the use of implicit imagery are visual metaphor and juxtaposition.

When calling images to mind from the moment of change in their story, a storyteller may select an aspect of the scene that stands out for them, but is not an explicit illustration of the event. For example, when sharing a story about losing a childhood home and describing the moment of change, a storyteller may find that a nearby tree, rather than the house itself, is the dominant image they call to mind. As they consider the significance of the tree in their story, they may discover that it represents the idea of stability in their life. The use of an image of a tree to convey stability in their story is a visual metaphor.

The images you choose and the way you combine them will work to create additional layers of meaning. The placement of one image followed by another to create a new layer of meaning is called juxtaposition. An image of a house followed by an image of cardboard boxes, for example, conveys moving. However, until we know more of the story, we may not know if the message is really about loss, freedom, or maybe both. If the next image is an open road, this could represent freedom. Audiences "read" the juxtaposition of visual images as having implicit meaning that goes beyond what one of the other images explicitly means on its own.

A limitation of material can spark creativity. A storyteller may not possess photos from the major scenes in his or her life. Most people have pictures of their weddings, but who has pictures of their divorce proceedings? Storytellers in our workshops may have only a few photos to work with, or none at all. But paying attention to the images that come to mind when initially sharing the story will help lead the way in creating a visual narrative. And although production time of new material is limited in our workshops, if storytellers are clear about what they want to create, then taking pictures, shooting short segments of video footage, or drawing and scanning images are all good options.

The length of our workshops is typically limited to about 3–5 days. This constraint on time can help the creative process, but it can also lead to choices about images that are less often considered than the words they accompany. For example, composing a visual narrative with images grabbed from an Internet search can be a quick solution, but oftentimes these images can take away from the integrity of the story. But more importantly, if storytellers have not allowed time early on to see how their images can do some of the heavy lifting of storytelling, they may find they would have altered their script to work with the images they ultimately use.

Well-chosen images act as mediators between the narrative and the audience. As stated in earlier discussions, audiences enjoy stories that lead them to a metaphorical river of meaning and require them to "jump in" in order to make their own connections. Images can grab the hands of the audience and show them the river's immensity. And images have the power to reveal something to the audience that words just can't say.

Step 5: Hearing Your Story

We've just looked at how visuals help bring a story to life. Now, let's look at sound. The recorded voice of the storyteller telling their story is what makes what we call a "digital story" a digital story—not a music video or narrated slideshow. By this point in the process, the emotional tone of the story has been identified, and sound is one of the best ways to convey that tone—through the way the voice-over is performed, the words that are spoken, and the ambient sound and music that work with the narrative. When considering the use of sound, we help storytellers by asking: "Beyond the recorded voiceover, would the story and the scenes within it be enhanced by the use of additional layers of sound? Would the use of ambient sound or music highlight the turning point in your story?"

In digital stories, voice not only tells a vital narrative but it also captures the essence of the narrator, their unique character, and their connection to the lived experience. One's voice is a truly great gift as it is a testament to one's fragility and strength. But why does voice matter so much? In a speech, for example, we are listening for an applause line. In a lecture, we are listening for the major points, or an outline of information. But in a story, we are listening for the shape of an organic, rhythmic quality that allows us to drift into reverie. Here we have a complex interaction between following the story and allowing the associative memories the story conjures up to flow around us. If an image acts as the hand that leads us into the river, the voice is the riverbed below our feet.

When writing a voice-over, it is important to remember that the piece, in its final form, will move from being words on the page to being spoken aloud. And unlike a speech or spoken-word performance, this spoken narration will exist within a digital story complete with accompanying images and possibly other layers of sound. Because of this film-like format, storytellers want to pay special attention to their choice of words and phrasing and the impact they will have. Less is often more, both in descriptive detail, and in the formality of language. This form is served well by the storyteller mimicking how they speak when they tell a story to a friend, unscripted and unrehearsed, for the first time after having just experienced it. They use incomplete or broken sentences, interrupted thoughts, and a haunting precision of choice words that make the details come alive for both the teller and listener. The more the spoken voice is inserted into the written script, the more the qualities of a person will come across and pull the audience into the story.

Digital stories that have the recorded voice as the only audio track can be tremendously powerful at conveying tone and meaning. When considering whether or not to add layers of sound, we help storytellers approach the process by starting with as little additional sound as possible and then ask: "Is this enhancing the story, or taking away from it?" If it is enhancing the story, then add a little more and ask the question again. One way to add some sound is to think about the ambient sounds that come up when recalling the moment of change in the story. When we listen to the scenes in our stories, they may include sounds that exist in the background of everyday life––traffic, birds, airplanes, voices, for example. These types of sounds help create a sense of place for the audience. There is no question that ambient sound can add complexity to a story. They help to set the scene and feeling, and its addition helps the audience better understand the significance of a scene, especially if there is a dominant sound that best captures its essence. When creating these ambient sounds, it may be simplest to record them from the available sounds nearby rather than search for pre-existing recordings. Also, the use of your recorded voice or that of another person to create additional layers of ambient sound can be very powerful, yet very simple.

As with ambient sound, storytellers can consider how the minimal use of music can enhance a story by giving it rhythm and character. From an early age we become aware that music can alter our perception of visual information. We see how music in a film stirs up an emotional response very different from what the visual information inherently suggests. By trying out different pieces of music you can change not only the story's tone, but also its meaning and direction. The use of instrumental music, whatever the genre, can enhance the style and meaning of the story's text and visual narratives without competing with the voiceover. While popular lyrical music may work, mistakes are sometimes made in mixing the story of the song and the voiceover in a way that gives an unintended conflict of meaning. However, by intentionally juxtaposing the messages, you may create another layer of meaning that adds depth and complexity to your story.

In our experience, storytellers have an intuitive sense of the music that is appropriate for a digital story. People walk around with songs playing in their heads which can set the mood of one's day, change the way we perceive spaces and places, and establish a rhythm for our steps.

A Note on Copyright

Your writing, recorded voice and personal images belong to you. When you consider using others' music, you cross into the territory of deciding what should be the appropriate fair use of the copyrighted material. Put simply, whatever the music choice, honor it by providing a credit at the end of the piece. If you are going to make money directly or indirectly by the presentation or distribution of the piece you have created, then you should have the artist's permission to use the music. Fortunately there are a growing number of legal online music collections that provide free and affordable media, as well as software to assist you in designing a soundtrack that is wholly yours.

Step 6: Assembling Your Story

At this point in the process you have found and clarified what your story is about and how it sits with you today. You have also established the overall tone you want to convey. You've identified a moment of change and begun making choices about how to use visuals and sound to bring the story and scenes to life for your audience. Now you are ready to assemble your story by spreading out your notes and images and composing your script and storyboard. This requires answering two questions: How are you structuring the story? And, within that structure, how are the layers of visual and audio narratives working together? But those aren't simple questions. Where do you start? Let's look at the question of structure. You've identified the moment of change, but at what point in the story will it appear? Is it at the beginning, middle, end, or is it divided up at different points throughout the story? Or is it the entire story? What other details or scenes are necessary to provide context for the moment of change? And in what order will sequence all this information?

When we tell stories for the first time after we have just experienced an event, we may want to launch right in, but if we see a confused or disinterested look on our listener's face then we should know to stop and say, "Wait, let me back up. In order to appreciate what I'm telling you, you have to know this…" In essence, we understand that the listener is lacking some important information in order to "get it," and so we choose to provide our audience with a backstory, or exposition. In going back to fill in details for our audience, depending how well they know us and know our life's ongoing narrative, we may find ourselves believing that we need to tell them everything, but quickly realize that this is impossible. A complete telling of every bit of detail is never really "complete," and in the process we begin editing, choosing which details we feel are the most necessary to include in order to construct meaning. In this real-time editing process, we are absorbing our listener's experience and making many choices about where their interest is peaked, where they seem lost, and where they are with us on the journey.

This process of telling stories and reading the audience's reaction is critical to understanding story structure. It helps answer the questions: What are the necessary parts of my story? How will telling this part shape the story differently or take it in a different direction? Knowing which pieces of information are necessary to include allows us to then determine the best way to order those pieces and keep our audience engaged. As the storyteller, we know where the treasure (insight) is hidden, and we are giving our audience clues to find it.

The joy of storytelling comes in determining how much to tell them and at what point. As our narrative literacy progresses from the comprehension of nursery rhymes towards a more intricate understanding of complex narratives, we desire more subtlety in a story's form. As the audience, we are less likely to look for intended morals and spelled-out meanings, and will instead draw from it what we find important. But presenting the conflicts, problems, or unanswered questions with subtlety requires not only identifying the right conflict but the right amount of conflict.

Daniel Weinshenker describes building tension in a story's structure by using a cat analogy: When you are playing with a cat and holding a string for it to chase, if you make it too simple, it will get offended, or bored, and likely walk away. If you make it too difficult and never let it catch the string, then it will give up. But the joy in the game is finding the balance between making it just hard enough to challenge the cat, keeping him engaged in trying to catch the string, and letting him savor it when he does.

In other words, don't give away too much information all at once. Allow your audience to enjoy the challenge. And rather than establishing a chronological telling of events with the moment of change positioned as the story's climax, you might instead try moving the moment of change to the beginning with little or no context, which may leave the moment hanging to pique the interest of the audience, and then go back and fill in more and more details and scenes and allow the audience to piece together the meaning and resolution. However, to do this you need to pay special attention to your audience's experience. For example, if you begin the story with something provocative and don't reveal the piece that explains it until the end, you may need to remind the audience about the question in the first place so they can savor the ending.

Once the basic structure of the story is outlined, the next step is scripting and storyboarding, or in other words, laying out how the visual and audio narratives will complement each other over the duration of the piece to best tell the story. The most common approach that storytellers take to planning their story in our workshops is to write notes in the margins of their script in order to reference where certain images or sounds will occur. In the next chapter we discuss storyboarding in detail, and provide a sample template that includes a series of tracks that you can fill in with notes about the visuals and their effects, voice-over and sound. As you determine how your visual and audio narratives are working together within each of these layers, ask yourself: Do I want them to be redundant, complementary, juxtaposing, or disjunctive?

Considering the above question will not only help you determine how the various layers contribute to the story, but it will also help you economize each in relationship to one another. You can ask yourself: If I have an image that conveys my meaning better than words can, how can I use my words to tell another aspect of the scene? In digital stories, the way we combine the layers to convey meaning allows us to economize the presentation of information and lets our audience make the connections. For example, if we hear a phone ring and the storyteller says, "I held my breath as I got the news..." and we see a photo of a loved one fade to black, we may understand that the storyteller is conveying a sense of loss. This process of the audience understanding bits and pieces of information as a single idea is called "closure." And as we edit down our scripts and choose each of our images, we need to think about how we set up opportunities for the audience to provide closure with each layer of the story independently, as well as in relation to each other. Oftentimes, this means your script requires fewer words. In an effort to help our storytellers, we provide formal constraints in the production of their digital stories: A word count of 250–375, and fewer than twenty images or video segments. This type of creative limitation helps the storyteller figure out what's most important in his or her story, while also helping to organize their time in the production process.

Digital stories contain multiple visual and audio layers.

The visual layers are:
- The composition of a single image
- The combination of multiple images within a single frame, either through collage or fading over time
- The juxtaposition of a series of images over time
- Movement applied to a single image, either by panning or zooming or the juxtaposition of a series of cropped details from the whole image
- The use of text on screen in relation to visuals, spoken narration, or sound

The audio layers are:
- Recorded voice-over
- Recorded voice-over in relation to sound, either music or ambient sound
- Music alone or in contrast to another piece of music

After your story edits are assembled, pacing is one of the final considerations in creating a digital story because it requires an assessment of how all the layers of information are working over the entire length of the piece. When pacing your story, ask yourself: How does the pacing contribute to the story's meaning? How would pace, or rhythm, bring emphasis to the moment of change?

A story's rhythm conveys an added layer of meaning. A fast pace with quick edits and upbeat music can convey urgency. A slow pace with gradual transitions and extended shots may convey calmness. A mechanically paced story may work nicely for a piece about the monotony of an assembly line job, but for an adventure story it will flatten the experience of the joys and hardships that the audience is expecting to savor. Adjusting the pace of your story provides an opportunity for the audience to listen more clearly. Stories can move along at an even pace, stop to take a deep breath, and then proceed. Creating space for silence, for example, provides the audience with time for all layers of the story to be absorbed. Even if you think your story is paced too slowly, chances are your audience will appreciate more time than you think to allow their minds to explore the thoughts and emotions that are being stirred within them.

The assemblage of your story takes time, and isn't easy. However, our best advice is to keep it simple.

Step 7: Sharing Your Story

At this point in the process, the layers of the story have been assembled. Finding and clarifying the insight, and creating the digital story have taken the storyteller on a journey of self-understanding. The story and the insight it conveys may have evolved throughout the process. Therefore, it is important to take time now to revisit the context in which the story was initially described in order to determine the relevant information to include when the story is being shared. To help storytellers do this, we ask: "Who is your audience? What was your purpose in creating the story? Has the purpose shifted during the process of creating the piece? In what presentation will your digital story be viewed? And what life will the story have after it's completed?"

Before the final version is exported, consider the audience once more, but this time in terms of how you will *present* the digital story. You may be planning to show your it to one individual, one time, for a specific reason. Or you may be planning to share it online with as many people as possible. But for most storytellers their plans fall somewhere in between, or they may not yet know the full extent that they will eventually share their story. But in any event, it's important to consider the contextualizing information you want to convey to your audience, both as part of the digital story and alongside it.

During our workshops we ask if storytellers want to say anything before their story is screened. Some say, "No, I'll let the story speak for itself," and others tell a bit more in order to set it up. When we share stories on our own website we provide a short description of the story and the storyteller's responses to a few questions: *Tell us a little about yourself. Why did you choose this story to tell? How have you changed as a result of telling this story?*

Knowing more about the story, the storyteller, or both, can reveal a new depth of appreciation by the audience. For example, the First Interlude of this book features Monte Hallis' Tanya, a story about how Monte discovers the meaning of friendship through knowing Tanya during her fight with AIDS. The backstory she provided in person before her story was screened at the workshop was that Tanya had passed away. The story around a piece changes and expands over time. In another example, the Fourth Interlude of this book highlights a young man's story about the sacrifices his immigrant grandparents made in order to provide a better life for their family in a small town in Texas. The story ends with a photo of the storyteller in his cap and gown but the back-story reveals that he was accepted to Brown University and returned to mentor young people in his hometown.

Considering your audience at this point in the production process may alter how you complete the final edits. If you know who the audience will be for your piece and what they know about you, then it will help determine how much context you decide to provide about the story. Contextualizing information can be either within or outside of the story's script. If your intended audience already knows certain details about you and your story, then it will help determine which details you include in your script, and which details can instead be revealed through outside contextualizing information. You may choose to contextualize the story outside of the script, but still within the actual piece, by providing a title screen at the beginning and text screens at either the beginning or end that display additional information. This is a common technique used in films in order to set up a story, or communicate what happened to a character or situation thereafter.

Being clear about your purpose in creating the story and how it may have shifted during the process of creating the piece will help you determine how you present and share your story. In our programmatic custom workshops, sometimes the storytellers are recruited with the understanding that their stories will address a certain topic and be presented in a specific context. For example, in a project with foster youth, their host organization may ask if they would like to participate in a workshop in which they tell a personal story about their idea of the "permanency" of family, and have their story be included in a training program for social workers. The storytellers are informed about the expectation before agreeing to attend the workshop. And within the workshop, they are invited to share their larger life story during the first of two Story Circles. Then during a second Story Circle they focus their story in a way that is meaningful and timely to them, and also addresses the specific purpose with which the stories will be to shared. Knowing that their story will have this additional audience and purpose will help them appropriately frame their story. In the interviews that follow in this book, Thenmozhi Soundararajan and Amy Hill both discuss the issue of presenting stories within their intended context.

If you know the presentation setting in which your audience will view your digital story, then it will help you determine what kind of contextualizing materials should accompany the piece, and will also provide more time during the digital story to focus on other content in the story. For example, if a storyteller makes a story about the successes of their afterschool program with the intention of presenting it on their organization's website, they know that the audience will be able to learn more by exploring the information online, and therefore won't need be concerned with including it in the digital story.

Whether your piece will be integrated into a live or published presentation, or is but one in a series of related digital stories that you create, or one that acts as a prompt to elicit others' stories, it is wise to prepare in advance by thinking through all of the possibilities as your story goes forth to live its life.

Finally

The storytelling process is a journey. And in our workshops, we approach this journey as a facilitated *group* process. We believe that the connections made between people in the Story Circle help to focus and inspire each individual throughout the process. For many of the storytellers we help, the digital story they create in our workshops may be the *only* digital story they ever make, in part because overcoming the challenge of finding and clarifying the insights and emotions in their story is not easily done alone. Therefore, we recommend that digital storytellers connect with others to share ideas and work through these steps together.

Second Interlude

Burning Memories

What can we say about our grandmothers? That they were nice to us, they sang to us, and they smelled of Juicy Fruit and Pond's cold cream and watched the "Wheel of Fortune?" That they wrapped everything in plastic baggies and pinched our thighs?

What about what they did to our mothers? Mine was always so sweet to me but I remember the time when Mom and I met her at the airport and before she sat down her valise, she looked my mom up and down and said, "You know Debbie, you'd be very pretty if you had larger breasts."

My mom was almost 40-years-old.

Years later, we talked about it. My mom would try to laugh some and say that her mother, my grandmother, was crazy.

"Your feet are too bony..."

"You look like a stick..."

"No man is going to want that..."

"You should wear falsies, like I do..."

She would beat her with a hair brush and drag her around the house by her braids. After one such event, my mother went into the bathroom, took a pair of scissors from the medicine cabinet and cut them off.

We sat on the couch and tried to figure out how not to care so much about what our mothers said. She showed me her high school picture. We looked at it and I told her how beautiful she was.

She had never known.

This spring my mother and I are going to the California coast.

We are going to take the doll my grandmother always compared her to... and burn it.

Falsies
—Daniel Weinshenker

© 1999 Daniel Weinshenker. Images and text all rights reserved.

Once in awhile I am stunned by the simple first reading of a script.

We were sitting around the table in our small lab at UC Berkeley in the Fall of 1999 with the usual assortment of interesting participants: a preacher from Portland, a drag queen from San Francisco, a couple of elementary school teachers, and three representatives of a dot-com company. We were heading around the table and this cool looking dot-com dude from Colorado sheepishly introduces himself. "I am not really a visual guy, and the script is bit short, and…" The normal list of excuses.

Then he reads. Wow.

The quality of his delivery was part of the impact. He knew how to read, and I was not surprised to find that Daniel was both trained as, and considered himself, a poet. But there was something else, a sense of release in the way the words and ideas reveal themselves. It was also some old-fashioned courage.

The finished digital story was even more effective. He made it sing.

As I have shared this piece, I have seen a wave of recognition come across people's faces as they remember their own losses, their own disappointments— the worst kinds of injury, the ones that leave the deepest scars—because it came from someone they most loved.

We all have stories like these. We really must share them. Or we cannot heal.

5 Approaches to The Scripting Process

Prompts and Processes

After the first year of offering digital storytelling workshops in 1994, Nina and I saw the need to closely examine how people approached the writing process for their digital stories. Just because the subject matter was clear to a workshop participant, it wasn't always easy to get the script written. In the last chapter we discussed the insights and structure for your story, as well as the considerations for working with multiple forms of media. In this chapter we will discuss the notion of how to find your best creative voice for self-expression in writing, about how writing happens, and about what makes the way you write unique and powerful.

As with our approach to digital storytelling in general, we find that our practice is ideally suited to group settings. And while you can use these ideas to get started on your own, success happens just as often by comparing your work to others, and by hearing a variety of examples. So find a few friends, declare yourself a writer's group, gather once-a-week for a month, and share your writing. Your digital story will thank you for your efforts.

Our Friend, the 4 x 6 Index Card

Of all the suggestions that we have made in helping people to prepare their writing, the use of 4 x 6 index cards has garnered the most praise.

The idea is simple: Novice and experienced writers alike inevitably suffer from a malady aptly called "blank page syndrome." The weight of filling a blank page, or more than likely, many pages, can easily crush our creative initiative, and as a result, cause us some difficulty in getting started. In our workshops, when we have found a person blankly staring at their monitors with a deer-in-the-headlights look in their eye, we like to hand them a 4 x 6 index card and say, "You have 10 minutes and only the space on the front and back of this card to create a draft of your story. Write whatever comes out and don't stop until either the time or the card runs out." We might also give them a prompt: "This is a post card. Choose a person that you think this story is for and write them a postcard about the story. Start with, 'Dear _____.'"

The card is small, and it is finite. It seems possible, and perhaps even easy to fill. So for the novice, in other words, we are saying, "Just get this much down, and we'll work from there." And for writers confident in their ability to write countless pages of prose, this excercise is a creative challenge. To them, we say, "We know you could write a novel, now just try and say it in only this much space."

One of my favorite Mark Twain quotes is from a letter that he wrote to a friend: "Forgive me, this is a long letter. I would have written you a short letter, but I didn't have the time."

Shorter isn't always easier for the mature writer. The 4 x 6 card also helps condense the narrative by breaking the story down to its most basic elements and forcing a writer to ask, "What are my choices in the beginning? How quickly must I get into the action of the narrative?" Usually, this approach means sacrificing the long exposition that accompanies the first draft of a story. But in the end, if the writing is no longer than the front and back of a 4 x 6 card, or one double-spaced, typewritten page, it ensures that the writing will lead to a two-to-three minute story complete with narration.

Writing Exercises

In a group process, we are proponents of writing exercises. While we are fully aware of the potential and beauty of free writing, it's important to have a class spend ten to twenty minutes writing down whatever comes to their mind. I have found that the shared themes and ideas of a prompted idea can connect people to each other in wonderful ways.

This is my favorite prompt:

> In our lives there are moments, decisive moments, when the direction of our lives was pointed in a given direction, and because of the events of this moment, we are going in another direction. Poet Robert Frost shared this concept simply as "The Road Not Taken". The date of a major achievement, the time there was a particularly bad setback, the experiences of meeting a special person, the birth of a child, the end of a relationship, or the death of a loved one are all examples of these fork-in-the-road experiences. Right now, at this second, write about a decisive moment in your life. You have ten minutes.

The writing that comes from this prompt, when it comes unannounced at the beginning of a workshop, often goes straight to the emotional core of the author's life. The act of sharing of these kinds of stories can be instantly bonding for a group.

If the goal of the exercise is to prompt distant memories, we have not found a better approach than theorist Bill Roorbach's idea of having participants in the workshop first draw a map of the neighborhood where they grew up. Reaching back in one's memory to locate the layout of the streets, where friends lived, the names of friendly or strange neighbors, the way to the store, or the secret paths to school, inevitably opens up an infinite number of possible stories. The physicalization of a memory, trying to remember a time by remembering the places of that time, the places you traveled through on a daily basis, a neighborhood, a house, or a room, usually leads quickly to events that are rich with the kinds of meaningful inspections that make good stories.

There are innumerable prompts that might work for various situations. Here is a short list of some themes for which prompts could also be built for powerful stories. Books about writing are filled with these exercises, so don't forget to pick up a few when it's time to delve deeper into your interest in writing beyond he digital storytelling experience:

- Tell the story of a mentor or hero in your life.
- Tell the story of a time when "it just didn't work"—a point, at your job or at some other event or activity, when you would've been typically competent or successful, and how that all changed when everything fell apart before your eyes.
- Describe a time when you felt really scared.
- Tell the story of a "first"—first kiss, first day on a job, first time trying something really difficult, the first time your heard a favorite song, etc.
- And of course, the old standby: What was the most embarrassing thing that ever happened to you?

These Stories from These Pictures

Digital stories often start with the pictures. Our easiest direction to anyone thinking about making a digital story is to look around his or her house and find images that provoke memories and stories that are meaningful. Then, see if there are other images around the house that are part of that story. And in the end, you will try to connect the memories that link all of these images together.

As we talk about storyboarding and structure, the notion of illustrating the script, or accentuating the writing with images, is emphasized as an outgrowth of a successful draft of the narrative. However, some people that come to the workshop have taken the absolutely opposite approach to the process. They will pull out the photos for their story, arrange them on a table, and sort them out in order from beginning to end. Then, with the story visually organized, they start writing. Is this approach effective? Of course it can be—great stories have emerged through this process.

Our only caveat regarding this approach is to consider whether or not responding to the images alone will leave out parts of a story that were never captured in any of your images. If you find that you would like to see an image in your story that you don't have available, you can look to an illustration, or appropriately implicit or metaphorical images to capture the sense of the writing that suit the purposes of your story.

Getting into the Scene

When authors come to our digital storytelling workshops, we have them share first drafts and talk about their ideas for their stories. Oftentimes, I find myself discussing the notion of scene with the authors. As an example, I can take one approach to my own story about my father's death:

> *Well first of all, let me just say, I was seventeen at the time and I had finished high school that summer. My dad had smoked three-packs-a-day, and had been trying to quit smoking for a couple of months. He was sixty-one, and had a difficult life as a union organizer working in Texas and throughout the South. But we had gone on a vacation the month before and he seemed like he was doing okay.*
>
> *He came down from his bedroom saying that he had a terrible pain.*
>
> *We called the doctor. The doctor said that it was probably an ulcer attack. He had had several of those. We waited. He got much worse. We decided to rush him to the hospital. It was a heart attack. He died within a half-hour. My mom was hysterical. It was a night I will always remember.*

What we have is a fairly typical set of expository contexts, and a sequence of events that most people use to casually recall a major catastrophe in their lives. This approach is a fairly direct and distanced recitation of the facts, and it usually finishes with a statement that is conclusive. In this example, the recalled memory is understated and obvious to the extreme. If this were a dramatic dialogue, a speech by an actor pretending to be natural, it would be fine.

But here is a description of the same memory that I shared at my mother's memorial in 2001, twenty-seven years after my father died:

> *I will never forget the sound of my mom's voice when the doctor said, "George is dead."*

"God No! No! No!"

A scream. A release. An explosion.

The sound of her wail bounced off all the walls of the emergency room at Presbyterian Hospital in Dallas, bounced down the streets and through the trees, bounced out into the night sky, all the way across the universe of my young mind.

In a single moment, a single pronouncement, everything changed for my mom. It divided her life in two, and it taught me that love can reach down into the cellular essence of awareness, and with its rupture, tear a human being in half.

What differentiates these two texts for me is the fact that in the second text, I am asking my audience to immediately journey in time with me to the exact instant when it all really happened. No context, other than the assumption that "George" must be someone really important, and the feelings, best as I remembered them, that accompanied the defining moment of the experience; my mom's reaction to the doctor's words. And finally, with over twenty-five years of perspective, what that means to me now.

In the above example, I tried to take the audience into the scene at the hospital. I could have described the way it looked and smelled, where we were standing moments before the doctor came up, and what happened afterwards, but all of that was assumed when I said it was the moment that my father was pronounced dead. Instead, it serviced the quality of the writing to strip away all of the descriptive material. We have found that audiences really can build an elaborate understanding of the story if they can get a sense of the pretext of an event. Furthermore, we know that much of what seems like important background, or exposition, is in fact superfluous to what really happened and what it really felt like to be there.

Taking the audience to the moment of an important scene, one that either initiates or concludes your tale, and putting them in your shoes, is why we listen to the story. We want to know how characters react. We want to imagine ourselves there as participants or witnesses, and we want to know what someone else takes away from the experience and uses to lead their own lives forward.

This idea of scene-placement is related but separate from the terms of the specific disciplines of literature, theater and film. Dramatic scenes all have complex sets of conventions that allow us to observe the action of characters within a continuous time of the narrative. In our thinking about scene, we want to encourage people to share at least one portion of their narrative as a scene—to write as if they were there, inside the events as they unfolded, experiencing the shock, surprise, or amusement, for example, for the first time. For many stories, this strips away the superficial consideration of the events, and gets to the heart of the matter.

Character Studies and Personal Story

We know that most of our parents are multi-faceted, complex humans. In one story, it may serve to have the parent in the classic role of the ideal mentor, thereby filling one stereotype of parenthood. In another story, the parent may be a beast, or display beastly behavior, but if we are mature enough, and we are given one small nugget of context, for example: "When they got drunk, they would be mean," it is sufficient for us to imagine that they had good days as well. We are probably aware that the story is a cautionary tale about human behavior, not the evidence to indict the guilty party.

Lagos Egri, author of the bible of my training in dramatic theory, *The Art of Dramatic Writing*, reduced all great storytelling and theater to the author's understanding of the true nature of the characters he invents in the world of his narrative. Like most people, when I watch a film or a play, I know when character development has been rendered ineffective when I am able to say to myself, "You know, that character would have never said those words, or behaved in that way." In any story, it simply will not work if both characters strengths and flaws do not drive the series of events forward, leading logically to the climactic clash or coming together that delivers the conclusion of the story.

When we write in the first person about real events and real people, we make the same choices as the fictional author, that is, describe those details of the character that are pertinent to the story. It is nothing short of egomaniacal to imagine that our characters are faithful portraits of actual people. In our digital stories, they are not even sketches, but rather, more like cartoons or contour drawings—brief and subtle outlines that highlight their most compelling, and relevant qualities.

Some of the writers that have participated in our workshops are fixated on elaborating their characters. They fear providing too simplistic a picture of the people they are describing, or their behavior in a given context, so they expand the narrative with a multiplicity of facets in order to feel more "fair." Personal storytellers are not judges or juries, they are witnesses. And as witnesses, we seek truth inside and around the simple lines of the sketch of their memories. We, the audience, are only capable of judging the approach they take to establishing the narrative, and whether or not their attitude and tone reflect balanced judgment or unreasonable accusation.

By letting the story dictate the degree to which we know the background of the character, we avoid cluttering some of the prose with assessments that cancel each other out. We can communicate which characteristic, for the purpose of the story, we can fill in with the broad brush of a stereotype sufficient enough for our small tale so the audience can fill in the character with the complexities of their own experiences.

Finally, A Few Words on Style

During my high school and early college days as a young journalist, I carried around a copy of *Elements of Style*, the William Strunk and E.B. White companion for all writers. I have to be frank, except for their call for economy, economy, economy, not much stuck in my sense of the rules of good style. In other words, I am the last person to teach anyone about formal issues of style. Having said that, Strunk and White might have been apoplectic at much of what I love in the styles of the writing of our students. What works, particularly as the words leave the page and are spoken by the authors, is not a case study in language usage according to conventions of grammar and syntax defended by the gatekeepers of the English—or any other—language.

What works is truth. By this, I mean that an author's truth about how he or she conceives of a personal way of storytelling *is* their style. How does truth happen in storytelling? Here is where the metaphor of journey, or quest, serves me best. Good writing has a destination and seeks the shortest path to the destination, but no shorter. The destination is usually the punch line, the pay-off, or the point of the story. Detours should never be accidental, unconscious, or indulgent. Each word and each apparent digression is critical to the final resolution of the characters' action. I am a traditionalist in this idea, having never fallen for what feels to me to be a experimental conceit of an "anything goes" approach to narrative.

But that is my truth. I have had the pleasure of hearing thousands of people share their stories, and each with their own style of telling. Some people like the journey along the road of their story, and the significant learning that happens along the way, rather than the arrival of a singular big lesson or a resulting moral. Other people love the wonderful mystery and elasticity of language, and what they mean by story is what I might mean by poetry. Other people find themselves hearing the sounds of words like music, and really are not concerned with the meaning of the words, per se, as much as the aural jazz of the presentation, for example, that creates a dominant tonal impression, and whose meaning is profoundly more complex than the simple "message" of the story. In that sense, I accept that when it works, it works.

The good news about those of us living at the beginning of the 21st century is that we have an awareness regarding how we *tell* our stories, and how it has much less impact than how we are *heard*. Stories do a number of things to people, but only a small part of what they do has to do with story content and our stylistic intentions. For example, when people hear a story, what is occurring in their lives at that moment that either focuses or distracts their attention? What is the context in which the story is being heard? What is the ambiance of the environment?

And who else is in the audience? Context at the time of viewing changes everything about a story and its impact.

We felt this in our own workshops after the fabulous release of the completion of a workshop, and the enormously transformative effect each story has on all of the participants cannot possibly translate to an audience that didn't share our Story Circle.

So trust your own voice—the way it feels right to you to put things, and your own approach to these stories. And make sure that when it comes time to share your story, you are certain that the context best suited to your story is being appreciated to its fullest.

The Author's Reflections on First-Person Narrative

Critics of our work suggest that our emphasis on first-person perspective cannot allow for hybrid forms of narrative that include combining storytelling with persuasion, argumentation, analysis, and dispassionate reflection. We readily concede that our work is a reaction to the swing of the communication pendulum over the last two centuries from sentiment to objectivity.

The Industrial Revolution established a model for breaking information down to little nuggets of data. That dissolution process, like many industrial processes, provides the constituent elements, but leaves out the soul of things: a tomato can be made in a lab, but who wants to eat it when offered a homegrown garden tomato instead. This process can be extended to writing in that we often analyze with dispassionate authority, but we miss the essence. Our heads become too separated from our hearts.

In the social and natural sciences, objective observation and neutral communication have proven impossible—we change the thing observed by observing it. We carry the ideological and subconscious baggage in all our thinking. A researcher or journalist can certainly synthesize, but the participant in the experience retains a privileged vantage point, and as audience, we want their narratives as unfiltered as possible, so that we can work through assessments from multiple perspectives.

From the very beginning we have believed in framing all narratives in the first person. This was simply more honest. Our unique perspective on experience is all we have, but it is just that. Our stories are not a doorway to truth, but they are one portal where light can fall through. And the more light, the better.

6 Storyboarding

A storyboard is a place to plan out a visual story in two dimensions. The first dimension is *time*: what happens first, next, and last. The second is *interaction*: how the the audio—the voice-over narrative of your story and the music—interacts with the images or video. In addition, a storyboard is also a notation of where and how visual effects such as transitions, animations, or compositional organization of the screen will be used.

Storyboarding in the film world is a high art bringing to life a vision of a scene. This composition includes imagining the many choices available to a director regarding camera placement, focal point, shot duration, possible edits, and camera-based effects such as panning and zooming. Storyboard artists combine illustration skills and a sense of stage business (where actors, props and sets are placed before the window of the camera), with cinematography and cinematic theory to write the roadmap for the director and film crew to organize every part of a film production.

The art of film storyboarding has taught anyone working on a story (from mega-movies to digital stories) one important lesson: Planning on paper will save the enormous expense of time, energy and money when it comes time to produce your work. Taking the time to organize your script in the context of a storyboard tells you what visual materials you require. If this exists, from the selection of images you have in your archive, then it just tells you the order of things and makes your edit go quickly. But much more importantly, especially for novice storytellers, storyboards clarify what you do not need, and saves you from scanning, photographing, shooting, designing, or recording things that don't fit into a particular story.

Recipe for Disaster

Our cautionary tale concerns Rick, just an average guy, getting ready to make his first digital story:

"What a great morning," thought Rick, stepping out his back door and going to the little studio he had cleared out of a corner in his garage. "Today, I become a filmmaker. I am going to make my first digital story this weekend. Today, I'll assemble all the material I need. Tomorrow, I'll edit it all together."

Rick's story was a tribute to his parents. Their 40th wedding anniversary was in a week, and he had a great idea about a retrospective on their lives. He had taken two large boxes of photos and a few old 8 mm films from his parent's home earlier in the week. He was confident that if he could just sort through the stuff, the story would write itself. "I know that's how Ken Burns does it, just gather all the sources and piece it together like a puzzle."

He had his computer fired up. He had a scanner and digital camera handy, and the video camera set up on a tripod next to the old 8 mm projector. He was going to project the film against a sheet he had hung on the wall and then record it. "Ingenious," he thought to himself.

The day began smoothly. Rick organized the photos into piles representing five decades of his parent's life together. "These are great," he thought. "I'll scan these eight from the 1950s, and these twelve from the 1960s, but the ones from the 1970s, when I was born, there are at least thirty of these I have got to use." And on it went. The piles grew, but no scanning yet. He broke for lunch.

Then came the film. "Old 8 mm film is really beautiful, isn't it?" he thought. "My parents are going to love this part when I had my first little swimming pool. Wow. I'll just transfer it all, and then make my selections tomorrow during the edit." Despite a few glitches in the camera, he eventually got it right, and by 4 pm, the video was recorded on the camera. He thought about taking notes about which sections were on his two-hour tape, but since he was having so much fun reminiscing he never got around to it.

"I have to find the right music—old show tunes and stuff. And I need a few archival images, and I bet I can find that stuff on the Internet." After dinner he got online, and around 11 pm his eyes grew tired and his hand had gone numb. But he had everything he needed—just all in one big folder on the computer.

Rick woke up in the middle of the night and opened his eyes. "...The part where they are looking out over the Grand Canyon ... I can cut to a shot of me digging myself into the sandbox when I was three. That will be so cool. I can't wait to start."

The next day, he scanned his images, played with Photoshop, and he captured so much video on his computer that he ran out of hard drive space. He played with his morphing software. He did everything but start on the story. Sunday evening came and it was still a big mess. The workweek was a nightmare, so he only had a few hours to actually edit.

When the event approached on Saturday, the best thing he came up with was an extended music video, fourteen minutes long, with whole sections of images, film and titles bumping, flipping, and gyrating for reasons unknown. Several of his parents' friends fell asleep during the showing, and at the end there was a spattering of applause. Rick attributed the reaction to the heaviness of the gravy on the chicken stroganoff that was served at the dinner.

His mother, of course, cried through the whole thing.

*His father, always supportive, thanked him, and said, "Rick, that was, well, really …
interesting."*

Digital stories have an advantage over film production—you are often using available material at the core of your project as opposed to creating all-new footage. But
as our story shows, the material itself can be profoundly compelling for the storyteller, particularly if it is a first visit in a long time. But without a script, and an idea
of how the story is told, composing a digital story can overwhelm the best of us.

Rick's tale is the worst-case scenario for the digital storyteller: So much wonderful content and so many cool tools to play with, but so few ideas for how things
will actually come together. We have met many people that have had symptoms
of these obsessions, and in our workshops, we work to try and gently bring them
back down to earth. We affirm that the material might seem irresistible, but we
encourage students to write a first draft and complete a bit of storyboard work
prior to diving into their family's photo archive.

Professional filmmakers use the storyboard as a critical production management tool, saving countless hours of experimentation by avoiding non-essential
material. We want to encourage our participants to reach for their highest level
of organization to maximize the precious time they have to create their stories.
For many of our workshop participants, life may give them only a few such opportunities to really mine the archive for the critical stories of their lives. But
we want to honor all different kinds of creative processes. For some, time is not so
extravagant a luxury. If you can afford to excavate your archive completely, to fully examine the creative palette of multimedia tools, and to work through a series of drafts
of your project to make a highly polished piece, the rewards are worth the effort.

Making a Storyboard

Our reference here is from a tutorial developed by the Center for Digital Storytelling in 1999 called *MomnotMom*, and is based on a reflection by staff member
Thenmozhi Soundararajan. The specific section that we refer to below consists of
a title, six photographs, and a short video clip. The soundtrack is a nice piece of
guitar music. We've laid out the storyboard on the following page.

Notice how few words of the voice-over are under each picture. Each line takes
about six to ten seconds to speak. In general, three to four seconds is about the
ideal length for any still image to appear on the screen. If it's too short, then it's
hard for the viewer to recognize what's being shown; too long, and boredom sets
in. If you're laying out your storyboard and find lines and lines of text under any
one picture, rethink your script or your images.

Images

Effects Fade In   Image PanImage Pan Image Pan   Image Pan

Transitions Cross Dissolve

Voiceover There is a picture of my mother that I always keep with me.   It is a curious photo, because in most photos I always imagine that people pose for the future, but in this time, this moment, this photograph, I feel like she is searching for her past.

Soundtrack Fade in   guitar chord progression

Images

Effects Alpha Channel Motion

Transitions Cross DissolveCross DissolveCross DissolveCross Dissolve

Voiceover Across oceans and between cultures, a young woman, a doctor, a wife, I think back to who she was as a girl,

Soundtrack guitar chord progression

Can the script be cut down, and can the image be left to fill-in for the missing words? If the text remains long, can more than one image illustrate the essential words? You may also want to use some effects to extend the viewer's interest in a single still image. But for now, try to use the best effect of all: letting images speak for themselves, and using words to say the rest.

Some Ways to Make Your Storyboard

1) Get a piece of posterboard, preferably large (22" x 17"), and a packet of Post-it notes. Sort out the image material you plan to use and label each of the Post-it notes with the name and, if needed, a phrase describing the image.

2) Create five or six horizontal rows across your posterboard, leaving room for writing text below each Post-it. Fill in the text of your script in pencil, and place the appropriate images above the appropriate words. The Post-its will allow you will allow you to move things around or take them out as need be and you can erase the text if you want to move it around.

3) Instead of labeling Post-its with the name of each image, you could go to a copy place and photocopy your photos. Tape or glue your copied images to the Post-its, and lay out your storyboard. The advantage here is that, just as on the computer, you can easily move things around.

4) If you'd like to work on a smaller page, photocopy the blank storyboard template on the next page or visit *storycenter.org/cookbook.html* and download the .pdf file.

5) If you are familiar with desktop publishing software like QuarkXPress or Adobe's PageMaker, or you know how to layout tables in Microsoft Word, and you know how to scan images, you can make your storyboard right on the computer.

Any of these methods will work. Do whatever is convenient and easy for you. A storyboard will speed up your work in many ways. It can show you where your voice-over should be cut before you record, and it may help you to determine if you have too many or too few images chosen before you begin scanning. Storyboarding is a valuable tool, and it can also be fun. Get others to join you in your storyboarding process and make it a collaborative project.

Images

Effects

Transitions

Voiceover

Soundtrack

Images

Effects

Transitions

Voiceover

Soundtrack

7 Designing in Digital

Working with Digital Imaging, Audio, and Video

W hat makes good design in a Digital Story? This is a loaded question. If you went to a design school, you would be handed a set of principles and conventions for good design. The principles would cover color theory, composition, perspective, typography, photography, cinematic theory, as well as conventions in animation and motion graphics, and a touch of audio design to boot.

For the digital storyteller, unless you are moving toward a professional career, you can save yourself a year of fundamentals classes by using the oldest principle in design: mimic what you like.

In our workshops, we show specific pieces in which the storytellers made choices that we felt worked with the overall impact of their story. Some issues of design including pacing, images, and soundtrack, are obviously integral to the seven steps discussed in *Chapter 4*. In this chapter, we look more closely at some design issues to expand the discussion. We will discuss two movies, with illustrations, to examine a number of choices that are fairly typical in the early stages of digital media design.

We will not be addressing how the pieces were created. Both examples were made using a mix of Adobe Photoshop and Adobe Premiere. The video and still cameras that were used offer a level of quality that are available at the consumer level today. We felt that offering tutorials in this book would make it out-of-date almost as soon as the book was printed, so our tutorials in current versions of software are available in our separate companion Digital Storytelling Cookbook for purchase at our website: *storycenter.org*.

Barbara French's *Redheads*

We start with a look at *Redheads*, a story from the first round of digital storytelling workshops in 1994 in our San Francisco studio. This piece was a collaboration between Barbara and her son, Dana Atchley, who has been previously mentioned in this book as the co-founder of Center for Digital Storytelling.

In many ways, we consider this a classic digital story as it is composed of a few small clips of video, and a large number of still images. Here is the script of *Redheads,* to give you a context for the story. If you want to see the movie, visit Dana's website at *nextexit.com.*

It might be hard for you to believe that I was once a little girl. I grew up in an old farmhouse in a small town on Lake Erie in western New York.

There were acres of grape vineyards behind our big barn ... and, one year, a field of strawberries beside the house. Down the lane was an apple tree that had three different kinds of apples on it.

My father went to his office at the grape juice factory every weekday and played golf on weekends. He believed in germs and we had to keep our hands clean and gargle a lot.

My mother managed the household, cooked good plain meals (and very good desserts), and took care of her three daughters Barbara (me), Martha, and Ann.

She was a handsome woman with a Roman nose, hazel eyes, pince-nez glasses and—wonder-of-wonders—Red Hair! She called it Titian and complained when the motor vehicle office made her use auburn on her driving license.

At the time of my birth she wrote a letter to my great aunts and signed it with my name. She wrote: "My father and I look so much alike. I'm awfully glad I haven't red hair like mother's."

I thought her red hair was really beautiful and I loved to brush and comb it. I often wished mine were like hers.

She died of cancer when I was seventeen. Her best friend asked the nurse to cut off her long braid, and she gave it to me. I have kept it for sixty-two years in a wooden box that says "Chocolate Shop, Los Angeles"—which is where my parents were married.

Eventually I had three daughters and a son—none with red hair. What a disappointment! Now I am the grandmother of six granddaughters—and two of them have red hair!

Redheads
—Barbara French, Dana Atchley, Megan Atchley

© 1994 Barbara French, Dana Atchley, Megan Atchley. Images and Text All Rights Reserved.

In designing the piece, Dana and Barbara had a number of choices that illustrate both common design feature sets in Adobe Photoshop and Adobe Premiere, and some good production principles of design.

Framing

As a videographer, Dana was experienced in the process of interviewing subjects and in framing video shots. In framing his mom in the first shot of the movie (*Figure 1*) he demonstrates a classic middle shot for an interview, from chest-up to just above the top of her head. He then allowed for a bit more room to the right of the frame, which allowed him to place the inset of her as a child.

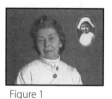

Figure 1

Figure 2

In other video shots in the movie, he made careful choices about how close he would move to the shot, capturing the braid (*Figure 2*), and apple (*Figure 3*), as tight as he felt he could go.

When you are interviewing a person, whether by video, or just taking a photo, consider carefully how you frame a person. A common mistake is to take the shot too far away from the person or object.

Figure 3

In the video at the beginning and end, Dana almost imperceptibly pans toward his mom with the camera. In general, it is a good idea to hold your shot steady, not moving the camera or zooming in or out. If you do use zooming, use it sparingly.

Lighting

Dana shot the video with a relatively bright light above-and-to-the-right of his mom, with another bit of softer light that was evenly alligned with her head and to her left. In lighting design, the notion of a key light to sharpen the features, and a fill light, to fill in the shadows, is a principal convention. Sometimes this can be done with lighting sources within the home, such as ambient outdoor light coming in through a window, which can often add a softer and more diffused tone, or even a lamp, which is more specular, and adds greater contrast. He also used a richly textured or high-contrast background that helped to bring his mom and other shots out from their respective backgrounds. Finding a nice backdrop, or one that is not too busy, but also not too boring, always makes the shot look better.

Audio Recording

Many people have come into our workshops with videos or interviews they captured with their home video camera. Often the audio is unusable. The most common mistake is setting up the camera across the room from someone, then zooming in on their faces to frame the shot. The standard built-in microphone on a home video camera takes sound from all directions and is quite sensitive, and as a result, the voice becomes lost in the room. Sound loss is even worse outdoors. The solution to this problem is to use either a "shotgun" microphone that only picks up the sounds that are immediately in the direction of the mic, or a lavaliere microphone that you clip onto the person's shirt so that it only picks up the voice of the person speaking.

When recording audio for voiceover, we provide a quiet, comfortable environment and supportive coaching of the performance with just the right amount of critique for people to optimize the performance as they record their text, get feedback, and rerecord until they are reasonably satisfied with the result. But we should not suggest this is easy. This may be the most difficult part of the process. Hearing our own voice recorded can be jarring. Recordings alter the way we hear not only the pitch, but also how we breathe, and enunciate certain letters or words. Most of all, we can hear when we feel stiff or unnatural. Fear and the lack of practice time result in believing that a straight reading is the only option. We all know what it feels like to be at a public event when someone reads a speech from beginning to end. It is downright uncomfortable. When we are nervous we hold our breath. The easiest way to improve a performance is to remember to breathe. As you are preparing to record, practice the reading aloud as if you were talking to a friend, imagine them sitting listening to you. The best part is that digital media is forgiving in its ability to be edited

Compositing in Video and Still Images

The first image (*Figure 1*) contrasts Dana's mom in her seventies, with the shot of her as a child in the shape of a cameo we could imagine came from her youth. We are quite used to this form of inset illustration from watching the talking heads on the news each night. The convention is quite effective—you have both the dynamism of the speaker, and the graphic information of the inset.

Figure 4

Putting images in layers on top of each other (*Figure 4*) is referred to as compositing. Composites can be as simple as a background and one image, or can be a complex collage of images stacked in interesting ways in relationship to each other. The compositing in video can also include elements like text, graphics, video within video, and animations. It is quite common to have the elements in motion as well, appearing over a series of backgrounds. The most important consideration in designing motion graphics and composited images is that the elements should service the story, and not detract from it. Making a screen too busy by covering up a wonderfully compelling image with other elements may be fun as an experiment, but it will distract vewers from the story structure.

Figure 5

In *Redheads*, text is used to provide information that isn't written into the script (*Figures 5* and *6*). The text is composed on the screen in a way that avoids taking away from important parts of the overall image, such as faces or other focal points. The composite elements move on to the screen and stay for a sufficient enough period to have them be recognized by the viewer, and usually extend through the end of the image. They do not tend to fly-on, fly-off, and bounce around the screen.

Figure 6

Also note that editing tools like Adobe Photoshop and Adobe Premiere give you the ability to add drop shadows to the elements which may assist in them being recognizable—as in text—but also providing three dimensions to the screen by separating the foreground and background objects.

Finally, color choices for text are critical in video; warm and light colors, oranges, yellows, silvers, or whites, will work in most circumstances. Avoid blues, reds, purples and darkened colors, even if you feel they would work in print reproduction. Watching text in these colors on a screen is difficult.

Panning and Zooming

No tool is more associated with our style of work than the ability for a computer editing program to easily pan and zoom across an image. Panning refers to moving across the horizontal plane of a film shot, and zooming is moving in or out from a point on the image.

Figure 7

Like any effect, panning should be practiced with restraint. Many first-time users find it irresistible, and pan and zoom on every image. In *Redheads*, Dana uses the generated pan only on two images, a house at the beginning, and the long pan on the profile of Barbara's mother (*Figure 7*). In each case, the focal point for the pan is providing an emphasis for the viewer.

We find that the use of pan and zoom is also a critical component in pacing. In *Redheads*, the edit pace is fairly dynamic until we reach the mother's profile shot. The zoom takes almost 20 seconds from beginning to end, and suddenly we are descending into the quiet heart of the emotional material. This long shot acts as a bridge between the expository material at the beginning and the context of Barbara's family in New York, and the story of the red hair. In this sense it shifts pace to focus on the information that we really need to consider in the story.

Transitions and the Blending of Imagery

Digital effects in video software almost always start with the ability to achieve a transition from one visual element to another. As such, the use of transitions is a strong tradition in an introductory digital video production workshop. The transition packages in a tool like Premiere includes 75 different transitions, from basic dissolves to peels, zooms, wipes, and slides.

If you watch television and film, you will rarely see the use of transitions—almost all of the edits cut from one edit to the next. The convention for when to use transitions in film is fairly straightforward. A dissolve is used, usually to or from black, to indicate the change of time and place, as from leaving one scene and going to the next. Other effects were developed to call attention to a cool visual effect in itself, as part of the style of the film. You may have seen the iris transition in old space-adventure serials like *Flash Gordon*; it is a circle, star, or rectangle opening or closing one scene to the next, a device that George Lucas brought forward in the *Star Wars* epics.

Figure 8

Because we are relying on static still-images, and because the style of our films can include a playful experimentation with what digital effects can show, transitions can come in handy. *Redheads* uses a number of transitions effectively; and again, the choice of transition is informed by the content of the images. In the beginning, there is a pan toward a garage, and as we get closer, the barn door transition opens up on a scene of the grape vineyards (*Figure 8*). Other wipe transitions are used that allow us, for a split second, to compare the current image with the image coming after.

Figure 9

But by far the most common transition is the dissolve, which demonstrates the notion of blending imagery that is quite common in digital media design. In photography, the idea of double exposing a negative is fairly familiar to most of us. The effects can often be extraordinary, with the ghost of one image contrasting with another to create a more evocative collage (*Figure 9*). Digital media allows us to play with the relative opacity of images and video with great ease. And it allows us to experiment with various mechanisms for blending images using color relationships, relative darkness and lightness values, and hue and saturation to draw out parts of an image over another.

The fluidity of this part of the digital media palette almost defies convention, as the effective permutations are seemingly endless. As with all effects, knowing when to stop messing with the composition, or frankly, when to leave well enough alone, are perhaps the more difficult choices for the designer.

Frank Gonzalez' *Bombast*

In 2000, we started what has become an annual workshop at the Art Center School of Design in Pasadena, California. In the first workshops, a short, experimental piece by Frank Gonzalez ended up as a discussion piece for our work, because it asks the question, "*Should we look back at these images and share stories with others? What right do they have to hear our intimate stories of pain and loss?*" even as it provides an intimate glimpse to Frank's own story. Here is the script.

I bought these old photographs for a quarter each, wondering what stories they might hold. 'Everyone has a story' they say. Me, well, I could tell you the one about my mom falling on her ass after trying to kick me when I was six. Or the one about my dad having to join the communist party in '71 in order to feed his family. Or the one about my sister dating a married man in New York City. I've had to live with these stories and I am constantly reminded of them. I don't want to make you sob, or put you in a moment in my world by telling you the one of me not telling my grandpa that I loved him when I knew he was dying. My dead grandpa would be turning on his grave—how dare you tell this story.

My memories have shaped me, made me who I am.

I wouldn't mind living inside the photos I bought at the market. A moment in time, no precursor, no story.

Bombast
—Frank Gonzalez

© 2000 Frank Gonzalez. Images and Text All Rights Reserved.

Film and Montage

Figure 10

Watching Frank's piece, you are immediately dropped into a series of loosely defined patterns—trees, underbrush, and grass (*Figure 10*)—that act as backgrounds for the discussion about to take place. Frank creates the sense that you are following the narrator into the woods, on a slightly surreal journey into his reflections.

Figure 11

No sooner does he establish this sense, that with his first words, we see a machine gun repetition of images (*Figures 11–13*). Twenty-seven image frames appear, each with a different part of four separate photos on-screen for no longer than 1/10th of a second. The effect is jarring, and in the one minute and twenty-one second piece he returns to this flashing of images six more times.

Figure 12

At times the flash of images is no more than subliminal. The relation of the content of the images to what is being said appears as a non sequitur, providing only more of that dreamlike quality. In closer examination, the content is of course related.

Figure 13

Video clips were used twice in a similar, choppy—image fashion, first again as part of the montage of non sequiturs, and second as a self-portrait that corresponds with the final part of the text.

Film montage works when an artist creates the conditions for the audience to absorb context, even as they excite and perhaps confuse us with visual non sequiturs. Even if there is an implicit relationship of the images that flash on or off, we cannot hope, at least on a single viewing, to create meaningful closure of their relationship. We are left with impressions, traces of the form and shape and substance of what we are seeing, that when it works, creates a dominant impression of meaning.

Frank uses both the bridge shots of tracking along the ground, and the camera spinning toward a canopy of branches to establish a continuity of the author's viewpoint on the moments. At least suppose that he is considering this narrative about personal images and his own life. He tells us that some of the images that are flashing are photos he found at a store. We view his use of non-sequitur and montage as part of the general unsettled tone of his writing.

When we write our stories, our first impulse is to provide the literal or explicit imagery that corresponds to what is being said. As in *Redheads*, when you hear "house by the lake," you see a house by the lake, and when you hear "apple trees," you see an apple, etc. But we, as a sophisticated and media-saturated audience, are quite familiar with film montage, because it is used extensively in television advertising and music videos.

Since our writing often doesn't correspond to a large number of our images, the notion of finding bridge material—images or video that provides a continuity of appropriate context but does not necessarily correspond to the story being told—can be a life saver.

Audio Design

Frank creates a dominant impression with his sound design as well. He suceeds in his choices of effect, a scratchy end-of-record on a turntable sound that sounds like crunching leaves, and the appropriate stark and foreboding ambient music, as well as his offhand and familiar performance of the script.

Most digital storytellers will not have the time for extravagant audio design, so the note here is again about restraint as much as effect. Sound effects can call attention to themselves in a big way, and they can break the rhythm in a work. Using an effect like a piece of music, a motif of barely audible laughter, or a soundbed of a low engine hum, on the level of almost imperceptible noise, will evoke their own subconscious responses. How they mix with music used, and the voice, is really the decision. When you are unclear, erring on the side of leaving it out is usually the best choice.

Necessity Is the Mother of Invention

The other design issue to discuss about Frank's film is the role of the experimental process. Frank chooses a story, a tone poem really, that can be illustrated with almost anything—any set of images. As an experimenter, Frank searched for both a subject and a method that allowed him to reach success in the shortest amount of time. Frank was like many of our students; he settled into the class slowly, and toward the end of the second day of the three-day process, switched gears and direction completely. Forget about storyboards and long research and planning processes—knock out the script and gather material as fast as humanly possible.

The images, as he suggests, are a random series of 1950's family shots and some contemporary artifacts that he could have easily had around him. All of the video is shot in and around the Pasadena campus. He has a few image effects, a blur filter here, and the colorization of his portrait video, but these aspects are quite limited. Nonetheless, his assemblage of the images in the edit happened quite quickly, because he saw the edit in his mind's eye.

Final Note

We have seen a great deal of creative brilliance in the face of the unwavering deadline of our workshops. This is one of the advantages of compressing this work into a few days. It is like using 4 x 6 cards as a writing tablet, and it forces us to strip away non-essential elements. We have found in our process, as well as in considering the processes of other artists, that often what is finished, polished, and refined becomes over-polished and over–refined and lacks the directness and spontaneity of the initial drafts.

Intuition is the largest part of experimentation. If most of our students stopped right after they completed their script, and meditated on the message of their work—the story's interrelationship to their entire way of looking at the world— and then went for a walk with a camera or video camera, they could successfully create an effective film just from the elements that would appear before them.

Perhaps this way of looking at digital storytelling is a bit too Zen, but it corresponds with our experience.

Third Interlude

From a Quiet Place

In 1913 my grandparents took a hunting trip in the Ozarks, shooting ground squirrels in blissful ignorance of the political turmoil in Europe. Within a year World War I would begin and my grandmother would give birth to the first of three daughters. She would outlive all of them. She survived these tragedies remarkably well with a vibrant imagination, a fondness for nonsense, and a total lack of self pity, admitting to grief but never to despair until her death at the age of 94. She had been born just days before the Battle of Wounded Knee.

My grandmother's father was a wallpaper importer in St. Louis, Missouri, a handsome man distinguished by his love of practical jokes.

His fortunes changed when the second of his warehouses, uninsured, burned to the ground, a tornado destroyed their home, and he fell under a streetcar, losing a leg. A strain of creative depression runs through the maternal side of my family, claiming the lives of some of its members, but never spoken of in polite company.

My father was the youngest and only son in a family of five daughters. His father was a baker who left Germany before the outbreak of World War I to avoid the draft. None of the men in my family ever wore a uniform. They avoided conscription through intellect, draft-dodging, luck, and conscientious objection.

Only one of my father's sisters married. Another, whose name I do not know, died young. When asked about her, my paternal grandmother would only remark, "She was a Gypsy." The genetics of this family were marred by strains of intellectual brilliance and Down's Syndrome, and a poorly developed sense of humor.

I am not the progeny of long suffering immigrants, nor of an oppressed race, a victim of neither holocaust nor war. My legacy is the flower of American innocence. I have inherited the photographic records of these families and their genetic code, but little else. Few stories accompany these snapshots of moments *in time, and like victims of war, or slavery, or genocide, I am forced to piece to-gether a puzzle where are all the pieces are scattered across a continent and all historians are dead.*

Nor do I have children to pass the puzzle on to. I am, to all intents and purposes, extinct.

Evolution
—Ann Jaeger

© 1998 Ann Jaeger. Images and text all rights reserved.

Among the clichés that inform our story mining is the one about, "still waters run deep." I have developed a tendency to look for the person who has only a few words to say in the Story Circle, who soldiers through the process disturbing the facilitators as little as possible.

My favorite story about this sort of experience occured during the 1998 Digital Storytelling Festival workshop at the meeting hall of Elk Avenue in Crested Butte, Colorado. The retreat nature of these "boot camps" meant a great deal of cama-raderie developed: people eating and drinking informally together, and sharing ideas, and collaborating. Ann was shy about these encounters, and Nina and I checked in once in awhile, but she seemed both technically and artistically self-determined. The other students were screaming for help, and it was the usual circus of craziness on the last day.

We had the computers aligned in a horseshoe. and when the time came to show the work, we followed the horseshoe around to the far end of the circle, where Ann was sitting. With each piece, there were the usual cheers and applause and good-natured ribbing. When Ann's piece played, there was a silence, one, two, three moments, and then a whoosh of exhalation as everyone shook their head, and then applauded. "Amazing," I remember saying.

I don't think this is a perfect piece of writing—although the design was visually pow-erful and Ann used music to a haunting effect. But her message, what it says about the author, and most importantly, what it says about American culture, is stunning.

I have a rap—a lecture—I share with people about how consumer culture affects story. I address how a mobile, international workforce caused the rupture of community, from San Bernadino to Sao Paulo, Bonn to Benin. I always think of this story, because it cap-tures this sense of profound alienation.

Ann has captured the dilemma. Free to make ourselves as individuals, we have evolved out of rooted memory. We, for all intents and purposes, are extinct.

Or are we? Stories like *Evolution*, as dark as they may seem, illuminate our options.

8 Digital Storytelling And the Public Speaker

P rofessional public speakers desire the intimacy, directness, dramatic tension, and transformational power of the storyteller. They want to move beyond the teleprompter, and beyond the PowerPoint presentation, to a rich and endlessly flexible presentation environment. They also aspire to a natural performance style: unassuming, conversational, and with as transparent a relationship to the technologies as possible.

In our work in digital storytelling, and in particular the experience of developing Dana Atchley's *Next Exit*, we addressed a number of these concerns. When Dana and I were rehearsing *Next Exit*, in San Francisco, one of the first issues we had to tackle was Dana's particular performance style. Dana was not trained as a theatrical performer. He didn't act. He told stories.

Dana was aware that he could not sustain a character shaped the way *Next Exit* was constructed. Dana's roots were in the singer/storyteller tradition made popular in the folk music revival of the sixties. *Next Exit* was constructed as a flexible playlist, each digital story functioning like a song. Between each story, Dana could intersperse a conversational storytelling style. Dana had sixty possible stories that he performed in any given show. The playlist was not entirely flexible: a beginning story, a number of bridge stories to the major themes or divisions of the show, and an ending story. This was to ensure that a dramatic arc was carried throughout the show.

Next Exit's computer interface also served as a transparent prompting device. By ordering his icons and then referring to and interacting with the events on the screen, Dana gained additional freedom to improvise and interact with the audience without losing his place in the show.

It is easy to see how this approach to storytelling relates directly to multimedia use in public speaking. Professionals who find themselves in public speaking capacities are not usually naturally gifted or trained actors. Acting is antithetical to their purpose. Their audiences want an authentic dialogue, not a performance.

Photograph by Jasper Johal

Dana Atchley performs *Next Exit* at the American Film Institute in February 1993.

In addition, most public speakers don't have the necessary time to memorize and rehearse their material, so they are forced to use prompting devices such as scripts, teleprompters, or the bullet points of the PowerPoint presentation. To the degree to which they are directly relying on any of these devices, they appear wooden, distant, and inauthentic to their audience. Using multimedia interfaces with icons to trigger bite-sized story elements is an obvious solution.

For the remainder of this chapter we will address in greater detail the issues of constructing a performance style similar to the one that formed *Next Exit.*

The Art of Storytelling: The Importance of Dialogue

Theater, public speaking, and storytelling all have a number of stagecraft elements in common. When we speak in front of people, we provide a number of layers of meaning beyond the text, through gesture, movement, tone, and language. Physical presence and speaking voice are a critical part of a successful performance. While these crafts can be honed to a high professional level, most of us learn essential parts of these skills from casual conversation and from watching other speakers or performers.

Theater, public speaking, and storytelling also share a rhetorical construction that reflects our awareness of the way oral transmission works with our memory. We have developed spoken word rhetorical styles of repetition, cadence, and cyclical design of the story to improve the audience's ability to remember and draw the appropriate meaning or message from the presentation.

But this is where similarity stops. Our choice in describing our work as "digital storytelling" has resonance beyond its humanist and folksy connotations. Storytelling, as defined by those who are its preservationists and practitioners, stands apart from theater and public speaking because it presumes a specific attention to the audience's role in shaping the performance.

> *"A key element of successful storytelling is dialogic. An audience at a storytelling event—as opposed to those listening to a prepared speech or play—justly expect their presence to help create a singular occasion. The story is not the same story it was when the storyteller practiced it before the concert began. A storyteller needs to acknowledge and adjust to, with some immediacy, the audience's responses, which provide a fresh and limitless source of energy, making each telling of the story a unique event."*
>
> —Carol Birch, *Who Says*

Actors and public speakers would argue equally that their awareness of audience alters each performance in imperceptible ways. But we are not only talking about adjusting a performance to enliven the audience or hamming up a joke for a particularly receptive audience. These are almost natural exchanges that the skilled speaker or theatrical performer develops over time. What Carol Birch and her storytelling colleagues are suggesting is that a skilled storyteller makes a total assessment of the audience and the specific environment at the moment of performance, and applies a conscious restructuring of the independent elements of the story to best suit the environment.

This sounds like a tall order, but it is more or less what we do in conversation. I arrive at a party. I have a group of stories in the back of my mind at any point, some current and topical, some old and situational, and as I bump into different people, in different situations, I adjust my stories. From the brief encounter, to the cross-table exchange, to the long and intimate discussion, I might tell the same story but adjust it unconsciously in length, emphasis, tone, and language. Our success at entertaining our friends and acquaintances is equally dependent on our listening and assessing our audience, as well as the degree to which we have mastered, memorized, and practiced the story segments we are prepared to recite.

The extension of this larger idea of storytelling as a dialogic and interactive process—rather than an instructive and linear process—to a new art of digital accessible, nonlinear multimedia data is that, in a funny way, it returns us to the nonlinearity and the interactivity, that define the organic way we have historically shared stories with one another.

I can imagine a large number of my friends who perform as solo actors, professional storytellers, and public speakers reading the argument above and shouting, "Joe, what the heck are you talking about? People want to sit back and hear a well-told story from beginning to end, and be swept up into my world. While I am sure I would be sensitive to how they are responding, I think the audience usually wants to be passive participants. If they want a conversation, they can come to a post-performance question-and-answer period."

And of course, the answer is, yes, audiences like to be swept up in story. But audiences are changing in two significant ways. First, as countless experts have noted, our attention span is getting shorter. We are a culture of channel surfers. The nascent popularity of stand-up comedy, improv, and episodic character-piece solo theater all direct anyone who is presenting on stage to examine why bite-sized narratives are particularly effective with today's audiences.

Secondly, as we move toward an interactive communications culture, we have an increased expectation that our communicators will provide the option of interaction. Broadcast media has responded to this expectation with the audience participatory talk show and, now, with Web sites and interactive games that invite interaction within the worlds or with the characters presented in the stories. In the live presentation environment, sensitivity to how you use your stories to engage participation, and the provocation of sharing of other people's stories, is increasingly desired. *Next Exit*'s most repeated praise was how the show invited the audience to feel that they too had a story to tell.

Digital Spectacle versus Digital Storytelling

In discussing storytelling as the metaphor for interactive presentation, we are also staking out a territory in direct contrast to the dominant use of multimedia in both theatrical and presentational contexts: the spectacle.

We all love spectacle—transportation into a story that is greater than our normative daily activities—humbles us and places us in a state of awe. Spectacle theater and circus has worked for 2,500 years. More recently, we've had 100 years of film, perhaps the most spectacular of all the media to date. Spectacle creates total sensory immersion, and in that state we are fairly pliant observers. Following in this tradition, multimedia in presentational environments often leans heavily on spectacular events, loud pulsating music, lots of projections, fast-moving edits, and flashing lights.

Spectacle is a low form of dramatic engagement. There are many instances when it's useful in shaping broad-brush messages that have singular meanings. However, public speakers usually have a more nuanced and complex intention for their messages. In our experience, the spectacular use of multimedia damages or obscures the message that the presenter was trying to put across because, most of the time, the spectacle only amplifies a thousandfold the paucity of content. In other words, there is a fine line between brevity and spectacle that must be acknowledged when creating multimedia stories. In our experience, we've found that down-to-earth storytelling persona offers a poignant approach to transporting an audience.

The Digital Prop

Isn't projected and amplified media inherently spectacular? Doesn't it automatically take away from the centrality of the singular storyteller on the stage?

This is a critical question. The art of storytelling often assumes the lack of device, nothing between you and your audience but your voice and your physical presence. One way storytellers further distinguish between themselves and theatrical artists is that they have a reduced concern for scenery, lighting, atmospheric music or sound effects that assist in creating mood in the stage production. The magic of storytellers is that they create all the effects from the incantations of their voices, words, and physical expression.

Storytellers have a long tradition of using props as visual and mnemonic devices. Multimedia in a storytelling or presentation context should assume the same role, and exist as a digital prop—a tactfully-used supplement to one's narrative.

What kinds of props are multimedia assets? When I was studying theater in college, my mentor, Travis Bogard, told me that there were three things with which actors should avoid sharing the stage: dogs, children, and fire. Multimedia falls into the fire category. If a storyteller lights a fire on stage, the audience turns its attention away from the storyteller and watches the fire. Similarly, large projections of text, high-resolution images, and video simply outperform the performer in terms of visceral attraction.

So it is true, we are dealing with a very powerful prop, and it can become either an effective aide or a distracting nuisance. How do we light a fire on stage while maintaining the attention of the audience?

In *Next Exit*, Dana Atchley did two things to guarantee that the focus of the performance remained on him and his story while using multimedia on stage. First, he created a separate visual setting for his role as performer. Dana came on and lit his video campfire, a little TV sitting on a pile of wood playing a tape loop of a fire. He sat on his only other set piece, a log, which was next to the fire. And when possible, he supplemented this with a spotlight on this specific scene. Dana was not immersed in the backdrop of his projection; he was in a separate space. His relationship to the screen was external, he pointed to it, he responded to it, but he was not "in" it.

Secondly, he used a wireless mouse to control the events on the screen via the projected interface that drove his show. This added another degree of focus on the performer. While Dana's videos and images were extraordinarily compelling, he could stop them at any point, reassert his presence, and focus on his conversation with the audience. The media was his prop, and he played with it as it suited any given performance. The fact that he rarely choose to interrupt the flow of his performance by starting and stopping is not the point. It is the evidence of his control of the media that sustained his centrality on stage.

The Computer as a Character

One step up from the performer's relationship to the computer as a flexible prop is introducing the computer's role as a character in the performance. Our friend, Mark Petrakis, another collaborator at the Institute for the Future, has suggested that true digital storytelling will not begin until we have well-designed interactive agents that will allow us to create a dramatic dialogue with our computers, both on stage and in everyday life.

We are all familiar with the prompting agents in a computer interface that pop up and direct action. It is not a big stretch to imagine an increasingly complex use of characterizations to expand a storyteller's options in adding comic relief and dramatic tension to the tale.

Facing the Demons

> "*Stage fright has been labeled the number one fear in America by a number of different books, including The Book of Lists. It ranks higher than the fear of war, disease, or snakes. Most people are more afraid of speaking in public than they are of death.*"
> —Bill Mooney and David Holt, *The Storyteller's Guide*

When I first read the above quote, I thought a great deal about who might be reading this book. And I thought about my work with Dana over the past ten years and our work as teachers of digital storytelling. When it comes down to it, we are trying to use the computing machine to address a fundamental conflict in the deepest recesses of of our souls. We all want to be heard, but most of us feel extremely ill at ease putting ourselves in a public position to be heard.

The vast literature of psychological and artistic self-help guides to storytelling and public speaking all spend a considerable time discussing ways to overcome stage fright. Besides the need to master your material, the emphasis of most of these guides is on your relationship to your audience. You should realize your audience is pulling for you. You should find a way to carry on a conversation with the audience, even if it means choosing a few friendly people to act as your conversational partners.

Performing is about skill, but it is also about natural charisma. Charisma is a quality that all of us have to a greater or lesser degree. Having worked with so many wonderful, creative people, I have come to believe that charisma is a function of empathy.

Many artists share a particular psychological approach to recovering from crisis or trauma. In many cases, their recovery from a traumatic event left them with a particular sensitivity to the suffering of others. For some, that sensitivity becomes an unconscious drive to enact suffering and recovery, again and again, in a public setting. This representation lies at the heart of dramatic experience.

When we, as artists, recount and express our personal journeys to and from personal crises, our confrontation helps us expose our vulnerabilities. Furthermore, by stating and confronting our fears, we invariably connect with our audience. We also invariably understand some of the reasons we are afraid to speak on stage in the first place.

9 The Story Circle

Process and Participation in the Digital Storytelling Workshop

Beginning with this chapter, and moving through the end of the book, we will be addressing the issues of facilitating a Digital Storytelling Workshop. Many of our workshops are aimed at encouraging educators and training professionals to adapt our methods to their particular practices. We approach our work as grassroots artists, and what we describe as methods are no more than practical values and principles that inform our practice. In sharing our experience, we hope to encourage a dialogue with our peers and the participants of our workshops about how we can continually expand and improve our efforts.

Going There

In 2000–2001, I mourned the passing of three of the most important people in my life. I eulogized them, stood witness with their community of friends about how much they had given the world, and sent their bodies to turn to ash. I spent most of my days going through the motions that my work and personal life required, but at least half of me was walking around in a constant internal dialogue with the dead, far away from this place, this world.

In June of 2001, I returned to a busy schedule after organizing the memorial for my mother, Latane Lambert, in Austin, Texas. As is the norm during the summer, a long line of workshops awaited me, stretching from the end of June through mid-September.

The first of these workshops consisted of a group of teachers who had been assembled as part of a year-long Fellowship program run by the Interactive University at Berkeley, California. They were a tremendous assembly from Oakland, Berkeley and San Francisco public schools. They all were warriors, and I was truly humbled at their commitment and endurance. We had a relatively luxurious seven days to work with them.

We approached the workshop with our colleague, Francesca Saveri, who was working on professional development and support in the Oakland schools. Together, we developed a number of writing exercises to help teachers look at their long-term professional goals, their professional inspirations, and also their previous year in the classroom. We not only wanted them to tell us what they thought was going well at school, but also, in the safety of the circle, to tell us about the days where they had failed or were frustrated. We were far enough away from their schools, and the school year, so that this sort of perspective was possible. Our goal was to have these writing prompts help them tell stories that would stand as assessments of their practice, and help encourage a dialogue between teachers.

On the first morning, we introduced everyone to each other, presented an overview to our work, our background, and a number of digital stories that illustrated various aspects of application and design success. We completed this showing just before lunch, and several of the participants asked me if I had created any stories. In response to this question, I knew of one that particularly called to me, and it was the memorial piece for my brother from the year before. I didn't really stop to think about it. I just went to my office, found the file, and put it up on the projector. What I hadn't thought about was how my piece might hit me at that moment, in front of all of those teachers.

So there it was, projected on that wall for everyone to see. And in that moment, I crumbled. I fell to the floor. And it was as close to a full sobbing release of emotions as I have ever experienced. Here, in front of a group of relative strangers, and as their teacher, and as the person in charge, I had lost it completely. And you know what? It was as natural as rain. The workshop went really well.

Sacred Time, Circles of Story

We do not pretend, at the Center for Digital Storytelling, to have license to function as therapeutic facilitators. The material that explains and markets our work does not suggest that this environment should be formally approached as a healing process. But it would be inconceivable, incomprehensible, and irresponsible if we did not recognize the emotional and spiritual consequence of this work.

As previously mentioned in this book, the forbearers of story circle traditions are indeed ancient, and they can be found in all cultures. They of course remain vital in the root cultures that survive to this day, and most certainly in the living traditions of our Native peoples and their ceremonies. Today, what we know is that when you gather people in a room, and listen, deeply listen, to what they are saying, and also, by example, encourage others to listen, magic happens.

The magic is simple. And we do not have many safe places to be heard. Sharing personal and reflective storytelling in a group is a privilege. In our culture, those of us who live fully in the modern world do not go easily into quietude and listening. We mainly talk at each other, not to each other. The result is the stressful sickness of modern living.

Looking at the Workshop Process

Like any classroom or group, each workshop is unique, and each facilitator has a distinct approach to their work that helps to shape the tone and feeling of their workshops. However, we have developed a basic timeline and tasklist that helps organize the process, and maintain a consistent attitude of nurturing and solemnity.

The typical digital storytelling workshop is three days long. On the first day we have an introduction process, an overview to digital storytelling, a story review and development session, and a Photoshop tutorial. Day two begins with an introduction to the video editing software. Then we move into a full production phase of the work which carries us through the rest of that day and through day three. The workshop ends with a presentation of everyone's work, typically on a large screen for all of the participants to watch together.

> To produce a digital movie, the production process involves four distinct steps:
>
> 1) **Importing material to the computer:** This involve scanning and digitizing audio and video either prior to or during the workshop. Recording the voice-over is a critical part of this process, and we usually insist on this being done in our lab in order to sustain quality.
>
> 2) **Preparing media:** In our situation, this typically consists of editing images in Photoshop. In a professional environment this might include pre-producing the audio and video work to enhance the quality of the original tape.
>
> 3) **The initial video edit or rough edit:** We encourage participants to first complete a rough cut of the movie that doesn't include transitions or special effects. The reason for this is that it allows the participant to have a general understanding of his or her piece. Furthermore, it helps identify the areas where images or video are insufficient for the edit.
>
> 4) **Special Effects, creating titles, audio mixing:** The final changes that are made in a digital story look to enhance the piece by using filters, transitions, motion graphics, compositing, audio layers, and text generation available in digital video editing software. Using these effects can be the most fun part of the project, but it is also where novice digital storytellers can become overwhelmed or lost in the possibilities. In order to prevent this from happening, we like to emphasize a specific set of tools that helps participants start simply at first, and then expand their creativity over time.

Project duration is an important parameter for the success of the workshop, and we suggest a goal of a three-to-five-minute digital story. In some cases when we know, for one reason or another, that the technical side of the workshop will be complicated, or the amount of time for preparation is limited, we suggest two-to-three minutes as a good target for a story. In order to help set these limitations, we suggest storytellers compose a script no longer that one to one-and-a-half double-spaced, typewritten pages. We also suggest that the participants limit their material to fifteen still images, and no more than two minutes of video.

At the beginning of our workshops, we make sure that introductions are comfortable and complete. We engage people who are feeling reticent about their participation, persuade those who give little personal background to talk more about themselves, or joke assuringly about everyone's shared fear and uncertainty in participation. In short, introductions help set the tone of the rest of the workshop.

The initial lectures that occur in a workshop are also a vital introduction to the group process because they demonstrate the credibility of CDS and the facilitator. Furthermore, they might help inspire the participants with ideas and examples for their own work. At each workshop, we assess the efficacy of our lessons and adjust accordingly. For example, if participants demonstrate an advanced proficiency in Final Cut Express, but have less experience with constructing a narrative arc, we would re-work our lectures to talk more about story structure and script writing, and spend less time going over how to place a transition between two images.

During the script review portion of the workshop, we like to encourage participants to share their story ideas. At this point, it's important to refer back to the original introductions, and consider who in the group might not be comfortable discussing their own work, or who might be intimidated by other participants' skills. As a general rule, we don't like to have the most outspoken or "talented" individuals go first because of their ability to intimidate other, less outgoing participants.

As facilitators, we like to lead by example and focus our attention on each story as it's being told. When a participant has the floor, we make sure we attentively engage with them; hearing their words and listening to the stories they may or *may not* be telling. We discourage interruptions, such as people talking, or working in another part of the room.

During the tutorial stage of the workshop, we teach the participants how to use the editing software in a way that mirrors the actual production process. For example, if we point out steps that the participants will need to follow to complete their work. The tutorials are a mix of information covering what is necessary, and what inspires creativity.

We have found that if we provide *just* the basics, or even facilitate the workshop based on a strict template, we may in fact make our job easier, but in turn stifle many participants' initiative and inspiration. We want their introduction to new media and storytelling to have a magical, transformative feeling. Furthermore, we also want to provide a broad range of tools that participants with the usual range of experience (novices to professionals) have an appropriate amount of toys with which to play.

In the production process, the true art of digital storytelling facilitation is seen when facilitators address each individual and each of his/her unique concerns. Each participant brings a different skill-set to the table, and it is up to the facilitator to work with what is available. However, there isn't always enough facilitator to go around, so we encourage participants to assist other participants if their skill level permits.

In the midst of these artistic processes, the maintenance and supervision of the computers, those unruly beasts that they are, is extremely important. We can assure all those who have tried to create a digital storytelling computer lab that the experience for the computers reaches a battlefield hospital proportion of symptoms, cures, work-arounds, and retirements. In fact, the battlefield hospital is an apt metaphor for the whole procedure.

Our facilitators chart workshop and participant progress formally throughout the various stages of the production, though side assessments by the facilitators are based on a triage approach to each student. Some participants will do just fine throughout the workshop and will require little attention. Other participants will succeed only if assistance is consistent throughout. And finally, and regrettably, we also have participants for whom no amount of intervention will result in a completed project on the deadline. When this final situation is the case, we work with them to ensure that their perspective on the process is as positive as possible. At this point, a student might be feeling dismayed about the accomplishments, and it is our job to help them work with what they have so they cannot walk away empty-handed.

And finally, the final showing of participant's pieces is the most critical and successful part of our workshop process. Before showing the films, we ask each participant to give comments about their efforts, and as we approach the appointed hour, the participants get to shed their anxieties.

As we bring the workshop to a close, we stop to recognize all that has been achieved. We also assure the participants that everyone would like additional time to complete their projects, and that each and everyone has a prerequisite disclaimer about the projects, regardless of their individual outcomes.

Many, many tears have been shed at these showings. The catharsis, the pride, the sense of awe at what others in the room have accomplished, and the resulting camaraderie, are all wonderfully satisfying outcomes of a successful workshop.

The circle is closed in this final process when the lead facilitator acknowledges the efforts of the participants, as well as other facilitators or volunteers that were involved.

Facilitating the Three Day Digital Storytelling Workshop

The facilitator's role in a CDS workshop is vital to the three–day experience. In many cases, it will be up to the facilitator to maintain a delicate balance between teacher and student–where one can offer the knowledge and support that is expected of a leader, but also provide a space for the unexpected.

Time management is a critical component of the facilitation process. Facilitators are careful about not being drawn too deeply into one project or group of projects at the sacrifice of others. As in most project-oriented classrooms, the facilitator must sustain an awareness of the general flow of each part of the process. For example, script writing and editing may take several hours, and may go over the alloted time. If and when this occurs, the duration of other tutorials need to be adjusted. Furthermore, time management over the course of three days, though sometimes chaotic, can be much easier than managing a timeline that extends over weeks and months. Logistically speaking, issues of file management and post-production, which are easily managed in short durations, become more complicated with time.

Many groups and businesses do not have the ability to hold multi-day intensive retreat sessions, and initial workshops may lead to once–weekly sessions that go on for months. However, more time generally equals less chaos, but what is lost in the longer forms of this process is the sense of daring, of impossibility, and the wonder, and the degree of elation that is compressed into three days.

The best workshop environment is created when distractions are minimized, and when participants can lose themselves in their work. When they are afforded this opportunity, participants tend to learn faster and retain more, as well as take artistic risks. But however you help others to facilitate a story, respect the process and the participant's efforts. In the end, a well managed process guarantees the best digital stories will come to life... and perhaps, live forever.

10 Applications of Digital Storytelling

O ver the last fifteen years, digital storytelling has been applied to many different contexts, and has encountered an enormous range of possibilities. In the following chapters, we present conversations with a group of practitioners in the context of community activism, violence prevention, public health, education, and business. As a preface, *Chapter 10* addresses the potential scope of this practice as it has been adapted to meet the needs of those in an ever-broadening range of fields.

Telling an Organization's Story

Whether you are working for a commercial enterprise or a civic group, trying to capture an organization's story is a common idea for a digital storytelling project. For some, the story is just another piece of marketing material, a step up from a PowerPoint presentation, but a step below spending $20,000 on a new promotional video. For others, the style of personal narrative in a piece that is produced with a minimal, but elegant design stands out as a new way of communicating meaning and values in relationship to the products or services the organization offers.

Our work in organizational storytelling has ranged from the smallest one-person consultations, to assisting marketing professionals working with large corporations. Dana Atchley has said that the thrust of organizational stories revolves around the question, what does the organization mean to you? And as the person whose work revolves around representing the organization, you need to have a good answer to this question. But no matter how good you are at making up reasons for your support, if your answer doesn't stir emotion or connect with an aspect of your life's calling, then in our book, you are not likely to be that effective in any of the materials you create.

Our approach always starts with a person's story that connects their own life experience to the organization's mission or brand. It may not be the story that makes it into your next speech, or the one that is showcased on your website, but until you share an experience with the audience, you won't be able to effectively represent other people's experiences and the resulting connection to the product.

Reflective Practice

We once had a student arrive at one of our open workshops in Berkeley who said that she was going to do a project about her boyfriend, and at the end of the movie, she wanted the final words to be a marriage proposal. It was our first marriage proposal digital story, and it told us that we had crossed yet another threshold with the potential of the form.

If we were to ask the students who come to our monthly workshops what brought them there, the majority would undoubtedly say they have a project due that is tied to some important part of their life—unique travel experiences or adventures, weddings, anniversaries, birthdays, memorials, work or academic achievements, etc. It is obvious, from our encounters, that digital storytelling serves these needs.

What is not so obvious is how digital storytelling works as a reflective practice. As storytellers, we have addressed how intimate our relationship is with many of our photos. We have also addressed the efficacy of story writing as a form of re-flection. But what is more complex is describing how video editing, particularly with the addition of photographic manipulation and special effects, is in itself a powerful new set of reflective tools.

We have observed that as people speak and write about, as well as manipulate their images, the photographs themselves come to life. This reanimation and plasticity of change helps the participant manage the meaning that their arti-facts take on for her/himself. In providing the space for these manipulations, the production process becomes regenerative in itself.

Health and Human Services

Everyday stories by local community members about pressing health and so-cial problems have become a valued source of information and inspiration for providers, educators, and policymakers. In 1999 we launched our public health and violence prevention work with the Silence Speaks program (see interview with Amy Hill). While the broader health sector was at first slow to recognize the power of sharing stories digitally, the application of our methods has proliferated at a startling rate (see interview with Pip Hardy/Tony Sumner).

Digital storytelling today has been employed not only as a tool for professional reflection, but also as a method for capturing intimate stories by service con-sumers. In the tradition of narrative medicine, for example, these stories assist providers in understanding the nuances of how race, class, language, and culture inform people's understanding of their own health and wellness in ways that are different from western medicine's views on illness.

At the community-based level, digital stories have played a critical role in social marketing campaigns for individual and community-wide behavioral change. For example, our work with the Partners for Fit Youth Network (PFY) in Santa Barbara, California, and a project on chronic disease prevention in Salinas, California, both have positioned local voices and images as the message bearers of critical health promotion information, as a way to prevent adolescent obesity and diabetes. From these two brief examples, it is clear that stories are being crafted and contextualized to point to the social determinants of ill health. Therefore, sharing this work on a larger scale enables public health advocates to call for health equity and highlight the ways in which inequities impact communities.

When compared to other service sectors the health sector has witnessed the greatest adoption of digital storytelling as a qualitative research methodology. Like Photovoice, for example, our process has been adapted as a form of community-based participatory research (CBPR) to examine the attitudes of young Latinas regarding pregnancy and mothering; barriers to breast cancer screening and treatment for rural women; and the role of traditional knowledge in health promotion among Alaska Native communities.

Whether the focus is on healing and reflection for providers and consumers, educating remote communities with relevant and meaningful story-based content, inspiring systemic change, or research/program evaluation, we know that the honest, first-person voices that arise from digital storytelling will continue to play a pivotal in the health and human services sectors in the years to come.

Intergenerational Connection

When we began our work at the Digital Clubhouse in Silicon Valley in 1996, we quickly discovered that digital storytelling was an excellent tool for fostering connections across generations. Since its inception, the Clubhouse was organized around a principle of serving a diverse cross-section of the South San Francisco Bay community, with an emphasis on seniors and youth. Since that time, a large number of senior focused workshops have been organized, including over a half dozen World War II Memories projects. The seniors bring the stories, the youth assist with multimedia production, and the middle generation acts as the organizational glue.

Cross-generational storytelling provides a platform for our elders to share stories community, especially for the younger populations. Instead of experiencing new technology as just a digital playground, they see the potential impact it can have for all people involved. Digital storytelling also affords young people the opportunity to confront frailty, aging, mortality and disability associated with aging. Furthermore, digital storytelling is also an appropriate adjunct to community or university-based oral history projects with elders.

Disability

It was also at the Digital Clubhouse where we began exploring the relevancy of digital storytelling practice for the many differently-abled people in our communities. One of our first projects was, "My Life As A Movie." The project was predicated on the fact that many high school-aged youth with disabilities face difficulties in finding appropriate part-time or full-time employment; we believe that providing these youth with a chance to create a digital reflection about their lives, their strengths, and their skills, could help them in their job search.

In the course of the workshop, we met many extraordinary youth, several of whom became an integral part of the Clubhouse youth program. We also were first familiarized with the advances in assistive technology that allow participants like Kevin Lichtenberg, who operated the computer using an infrared mouse/tracking device attached to his forehead, to design and create their own stories. Giving voice takes on new meaning when those with hearing disabilities can "see" their voice for the first time displayed as a waveform on a computer screen.

Since this time, we have had several opportunities to work with members of the disability community to develop digital stories. In particular, in our collaboration with Professor Sue Schweik at the University of California, Berkeley, and activist/artist Neil Marcus, we developed a digital storytelling component within a college course on Creative Writing and the Body. The class aimed to foster dialogue about disability and many of the larger cultural issues that are raised by our perceptions of self and our bodies. This meant confronting issues about the notion of limitation, and talking about how our stories are shaped whether we are perceived to be visibly whole, visibly limited, or invisibly limited in countless ways.

The stories of struggle, the stories of resolve, and the stories of frustration and beauty were captured elegantly in the digital storytelling process. The larger canon of literary and creative accomplishment coming from differently-abled communities continue to be served by various adaptations of digital storytelling processes.

Youth Programs

Three months after we started the San Francisco Digital Media Center in 1994, we found ourselves working with Ron Light, a local educational media expert, to develop D*LAB. D*LAB would remain a program of our center for almost four years, allowing us to sustain an active body of work with teens from throughout San Francisco's many diverse communities. In our projects we explored digital video stories, as well as web-based stories and special workshops with specific schools. Additionally, we looked at the Title IX program of the San Francisco Unified School District, and also worked with Native American youth.

Daniel Weinshenker's many years of working with the Downtown Area Visual Arts program leading youth through the process of developing high quality stories, has also demonstrated how youth can meet the challenge of writing meaningful and powerful prose. The 826 Center movement, Streetside Stories, the National Writing Projects' local youth programs, and many others, have made digital storytelling a critical part of youth media strategy.

These experiences affirmed our attitude that young people, despite feeling adept at multimedia tools, long for environments where freedom of expression is possible—where they can choose what story to tell and decide how it should be told. After-school environments are often where effective youth-based projects can best be developed. These efforts give youth a sense of real world consequence that is a critical component of a constructive educational philosophy. And for the most part, the students and instructors are not weighted down with the criteria of assessment and bureaucratic inertia that plagues many of our public school settings.

As has also been stated by a number of our colleagues working in the context of media literacy with youth, digital storytelling plays an ideal intermediary role between the observations and analysis of media (the classic media literacy curriculum), and full-on film and video production. We learn most about the way media affects us by manipulating media and making our own editing decisions.

Youth video, animation and film projects have for years demonstrated that the desire to speak in the language of film is virtually universal among young people. However, the expense in time and resources in organizing film production inhibits accessibility. Digital storytelling puts the participant in the editing chair with a minimal amount of preparation, and without the lengthy process of shooting, reviewing, capturing and working with video clips. Young people walk away from their first video-editing experience with a new set of eyes and ears, as they see how special effects and design decisions are constructed and work upon the minds of viewers.

With the commitment to educational technology use in classrooms and youth programs throughout the developed and developing worlds, digital storytelling and other forms of digital media publishing are becoming key parts of curricula and programming at many youth centers and after-school programs.

Identity and Diversity

African American historical leader W.E.B. Dubois' incandescent pronouncement that "The problem of the twentieth century is the problem of the color line," informs our work in the twenty-first century as well. Much of the discussions about digital divides, "serving those at-risk," and "cultural equity" are sophisticated euphemisms for discussions of race in the public sphere. No cultural work can be promulgated without addressing a point of view about race and other markers of identity.

Digital storytelling has been seen as a vector for two of the more complex aspects of this discussion. First and foremost from our point of view, people within every culture have the right to carry on conversations, form organizations, and amalgamate their own stories outside of the mainstream cultural discourse. Integration into a dominant society that sustains aspects of the legacies of genocide, segregation, and racism in many of its institutional practices is not the end goal of cultural pluralism. We have encouraged the development of programs to assist people within African-American, Latino, Asian-Pacific Islander, Native American and LGBTQ communities to capture their own stories, using approaches and methods that reflect both historical cultural practices and contemporary expressions and ideas within these communities. Our conversation with Thenmozhi Soundararajan in Chapter 11 addresses these issues in more detail.

As an example, we were involved in the Spring of 2001, through our associates China Ching and Thenmozhi Soundararajan, in a workshop with a group of Native Californian activists who were part of the Circle of Voices project. On principle, the workshop did not allow visitors or observers to attend, and the artifacts photographed for inclusion in stories, many of which represented sacred items to the various communities, were not shared with a community outside the circle of participants. As a final precaution, none of the associated digitized materials at the end of the project were allowed to remain at our center, nor were the stories distributed or exhibited in any fashion.

Another aspect of a culturally democratic practice is to provide media-based mechanisms for people who have felt excluded from the channels of economic and political access to share their stories publicly. We have encouraged all of our participants to imagine their stories as having broad relevancy to a larger public, and where appropriate, work directly with our collaborative partners to seek broadcast (radio and television) and other venues for distribution.

Inevitably, changing from an "I" point-of-view to a "we" becomes a more sensitive dialogue in these particular pieces that address racial and social justice. Giving witness as an individual coalesces with a sense of collective will, and with a view that suggests any document reporting on the conditions people face need also include a sense of collective responsibility.

Since our beginnings, we have sought to sustain a diversity of participation in our workshops held throughout the country. We have an ongoing scholarship and outreach effort to engage communities of color, and much of our specific work in public health, community development, and social services focuses on low-income and immigrant communities. When possible, we also provide pro bono technical and production support to the grassroots efforts of our colleagues working both locally and internationally.

Activism

While many dialogues about identity and diversity reflect a certain degree of activism, we see the implementation of digital storytelling as part of the community organizer's tool kit as having a unique set of considerations as well.

When my father arrived in a small, east Texas town to begin a labor-organizing project at the local garment factory, his first project was the creation of an agitational newsletter. The newsletter captured stories about what was going on in the plant, what abuses were being perpetrated by which managers, what plans the company had to keep employees in line, and what funny incidents demonstrated flashes of spontaneous resistance. He told stories, as much as possible, in the words of the folks living the experience.

In my own activist experience, while I prided myself on being able to knock out an effective, rabble-rousing speech, I knew what made my arguments for change and resistance effective were the most direct examples of courage and leadership that I had observed. Capturing these stories was what breathed life into our ideology.

Of course, part of the problem with political people on both the left and the right is that they often make sure that the stories projected suit their ideologies and political programs. The "politically correct" stories are the only ones that surface in their campaigns. In a long-range view, common sense suggests that the activist would do well to leave the sifting of arguments within a range of stories to the audience, and instead focus on facilitating voice and educational empowerment as broadly as possible.

Your own political stance aside, imagining how digital storytelling can be easily integrated into strategies for change is not difficult. In our own programs, we have worked with countless activists to develop projects that address the issues they care about so deeply, and the media has been presented as part of community meetings, assemblies, policymaking venues, political rallies and in organizing packages distributed to their constituents.

In addition, using the digital storytelling workshop as a team-building exercise has been shown to be effective. If the resources are available, gathering a group of organizers together to share their own stories and learn the process and tool set can orient and energize a campaign.

International Development

As our work spread from its initial base in California across oceans and continents, it began to find a place in the development sector, which for decades has explored and promoted the value of participatory communications strategies. With its emphasis on first-person narrative and meaningful involvement in the media production process, digital storytelling represents a user-friendly approach to participatory video, a method practiced widely in the context of international health and community development initiatives in Africa, South Asia, and Latin America.

Those involved in international projects face many challenges when implementing a storytelling process that is appropriate for resource-poor environments. For example, what adaptations are required for digital storytelling with individuals and communities that lack a written literacy or even a written version of their first language? And in terms cultural sensitivity, how does one approach issues related to representation, privacy, story ownership, and program sustainability in the context of colonialism and media exploitation–two factors that are pervasive in development work?

Our approach has been to emphasize partnerships with local NGOs well versed in the needs and issues of their area, and to push for work that goes well beyond the mere documentation of stories to integrate personal narrative into existing health and human rights agendas. Flexibility has been key to the success of projects in Uganda and South Africa, where we have brought testimonial practices into the process of story development, and worked closely with skilled interpreters to capture and edit the narratives of workshop participants. While digital story creators have historically relied on personal archives of photos and video clips to develop visual treatments for their stories, work in the development sector has required the integration of photography and artful creation for participants who lack such image collections.

An emphasis on organizational capacity building and sustainability has also characterized much of our international work. In Brazil, we trained staff at the Museu da Pessoa (Museum of the Person) on digital storytelling methods and supported them in adapting the process for a large-scale youth voice initiative. In South Africa, our ongoing collaboration with the Sonke Gender Justice Network has also involved facilitator training and mentoring for staff, as well as additional partnerships to ensure a long-term presence to support the continued evolution of the work throughout the region.

K–12 and Higher Education Curricula

Educators from K–12 schools as well as colleges and universities have been an integral part of our practice from the start. The leading proponents of educational technology for project-based learning identified digital storytelling as one of the most obvious and effective methods within a broad cross-section of curricular areas. Writing and voice, reflections on civic processes, oral histories, and essays on major subject areas are just some of the ways the work has been integrated into curriculums across grade levels.

We imagine a much broader role for digital storytelling in an integrated constructivist learning setting that easily could address science and math as well. We agree with the philosophy that if children remember the stories of their own learning processes and can readily apply their unique sets of strengths and intelligences, they will develop their own strategies for learning. Because it goes well beyond the facts and formulas they are expected to regurgitate as evidence of their mastery of knowledge, digital storytelling will service not only the academic success of students but also their life success.

Building a portfolio of how students approached problems through digital storytelling could provide a vivid and enjoyable mechanism for charting the development of their learning over time. Just imagine a student capping her/his educational career with an interactive performance of stories showing work on projects from kindergarten through college, and projecting them at the graduation party.

For educators at either the K-12 or college levels, learning not only how to facilitate digital storytelling but also how to articulate judgments about the design of video with the same authority they have in relation to text can take years of training and practice. But today, the necessary toolsets and the training of educators to use them have found their way into classrooms across the U.S. and around the world.

Scenario Planning/Futures Thinking

In 1997, we began a multi-year collaboration with the Menlo Park-based Institute for the Future (IFTF) to look at the role of digital storytelling in scenario development. IFTF has always integrated a narrative approach into its reporting methodology by combining essays that examine major technological trends with fictional scenarios involving characters as consumers and managers a decade or more into the future. They were also involved in looking at the ways that new media technologies could be more thoroughly integrated into knowledge management and organizational communication practices. Because digital storytelling fit so well with their own methodologies and practices, in 1998 they commissioned us to create a white paper on our work (several articles from this paper are excerpted in this book).

Of particular interest to us were a pair of projects involving educators and high school youth (2000), and then community members (2001), where IFTF and members of our staff collaborated on extended workshops to both educate participants about the implications of the trends being examined in IFTF research, and gather stories about their views of the future and the impact of technology on their lives.

In the work with educators and students, we were struck by the ability of each group to imagine the impact that technological progress would have on their personal and professional lives. With the community members who were also involved in a longer assessment of their then-current attitudes toward technology, we were impressed by the ease with which they imagined integrating the commitments and values they held most dear into a future, and with their ability to envision some of the enabling technologies on the horizon. In both cases, workshop participants recognized that technological progress had a Janus-like role in their lives, enabling and oppressing at the same time.

The stories themselves were surprisingly powerful, given that the style of speculative writing and the notion of illustrating the future in image was new to all participants. We found that the process assisted all of the participants in thinking more broadly about historical change in their communities. We hope to see the emergence of much more elaborate programs for capturing and developing stories about how individuals view their futures, as a process for initiating dialogue about large-scale community development and the impact of global climate change and other pressing issues.

Professional Reflection

Myriad approaches to periodic review and assessment exist within various professions and sectors. Management consultants in both the commercial and civic arenas have developed numerous ways to give organizations and individuals the opportunity to take stock of their development and morale. Storytelling opportunities have been presented in group settings, or as one-on-one dialogues. And as with any reflective practice, the process is usually more important than the product. Unfortunately, written reports usually disappear into files and filing cabinets and never again see the light of day and have little in the way of reflective substance.

In the last five years, we have witnessed interest among a growing number of professionals to use digital storytelling as a way to give the product of their assessment processes new and more enduring meaning. Capturing one's professional process over the course of a year as a classroom teacher, for example, with the production of a multimedia story as the final assessment piece, provides a wide array of topics to explore. The professional can look at her/his relationship to students by recording the students at work, or at their own development of new styles of teaching and testing by documenting themselves as teachers. They can also explore themes and issues around their personal life or the larger context of their school or district as a way of setting the backdrop for a story.

With a grant from the Spencer Foundation, we worked with the National Writing Project to collaborate with a group of rural educators from around the U.S. in a project to encourage this kind of assessment. The resulting stories have found their way into countless dialogues with other educators and have inspired numerous school districts to consider projects to capture the reflections of classroom teachers.

When stories are completed in an environment of shared reflection, they can inspire and lead to more in-depth reflections by the storytellers' peers. The portfolio of these teachers' stories offered a treasure trove of ethnographic detail, and in the case of NWP, valuable information about education and teaching. These multimedia stories provide an effective and entertaining way of presenting the arguments of administrators and managers about changes needed in organizational thinking.

Team Building

During the height of the dot com boom in the late nineties, hardly a week went by without a national news story about how project management professionals were busy cooking up "experiences" that would enable the members of teams to bond more closely. The examples included fire walking, rope courses, sports camps, extreme hiking, and other outdoor adventures.

Undoubtedly, people who are forced by circumstance to execute complex projects over intense periods will operate more effectively if they are initiated through an ego-stripping test of endurance and nerve. The physical test as a communal rite of passage is an ancient ritual.

But it would seem that the extremity of some of these experiences is perhaps a bit overstated for the relatively mundane application of the average professional project, no matter how stressful such a project may become. They also seem much more suited to a traditional view of male-dominated cultures where physical prowess and leadership are considered interchangeable.

A number of our clients in both civic and commercial organizations have suggested that the strongest application of our work is in amplifying the process of the personal story exchange. While developing intimacies through personal stories is a common part of informal professional life, storytelling circles, and the more intense production madness of a digital storytelling workshop, gets to the heart of the matter much more directly.

We have witnessed the solidarity that typically develops among people in the context of workshops, and while thus far this outcome has been unintended, we are watching with interest to see where and when it will be taken up and examined more fully.

Journalism

Particularly in the last five years, and since the advent of widely available high-bandwidth internet access, journalism has emerged as a sector that is exploring many innovative uses for digital storytelling. While it would seem that the journalistic profession is built on story, ethical concerns have tended to divorce authors' personal experiences from their treatment of stories. But for many of us, emotional content is at the heart of effective journalism.

Our colleague, Jane Stevens, formerly with the New York Times and now working as an independent science journalist, has developed her own approach and theories about new multimedia authorship for journalists. In this context, she approached us to collaborate on a few workshops to train some of her peers on digital storytelling practice.

Back in the late 1990s, Jane was one of the first people to correctly point out that the traditional divisions of labor between print journalists, photographers and video journalists were dissolving as more and more news was developed as entertainment. At the same time, online journalism and the number of freelance journalists were growing, and a much more complex relationship between journalists and audiences in the reporting of news resulted. Stevens continues to see journalists as both multimedia storytellers, often with recognizable personal styles, and news facilitators, working with sources that are helping to craft their own stories, and developing their own web-based platforms for sharing them.

Following the initial work with Jane, we were asked to train staff at the BBC on digital storytelling methods, and they subsequently launched a large-scale on-line broadcast initiative called *Capture Wales,* the first of many "citizen journalism" approaches to our methods to emerge.

Today, news outlets around the world offer incredibly sophisticated forms of multimedia-based online journalism, and YouTube collects and shares user-generated content that is equally popular. In our work, we continue to emphasize the value of first-person narrative, participatory production, and group processes for shaping and sharing meaningful stories. When these values align with journalism and other media outlets, both storytellers and viewers benefit immensely.

Technology Training

Ironically, technology training, perhaps the most obvious application for the skill set we use in digital storytelling, is in some ways the least interesting to us organizationally. We realize that the digital divide is alive and well along both socio-economic and cultural lines, as well as along lines of age and gender—both in the U.S. and throughout the world. Getting access to digital media production tool sets is far from a closed issue, especially as these discussions expand globally, so providing access is a critically important part of our work.

At the same time, we are not overly concerned about the ways that innumerable communities seeking access will ultimately be able to put their hands on the tools. As costs decrease, creative community solutions such as community-based technology access centers can pool their resources and service a large number of people. We also recognize that digital video/multimedia production and training curricula has been developed and refined over the years by a plethora of non-profit media centers, as well as colleges and universities, for people who want in-depth knowledge of the tools. Opportunities such as these may represent a better option than our workshops, which emphasize narrative and story rather than the intricacies of software use.

Digital Storytelling and Urban Planning

In the appendix on the World of Digital Storytelling, we discuss the potential of geographic information systems (GIS) like Google Earth and Google Maps. Countless opportunities now exist to integrate stories into places on a map, thereby realigning stories with their place-based origins. One of the most exciting uses of this material is related to community-based learning and urban planning. In the last five years, beginning with our collaboration with the Ukiah Players Theater, located in Mendocino County, we have been examining place-based storytelling in these contexts. In Houston, Texas; New Orleans, Louisiana; and Tuscaloosa, Alabama, we worked on a prototype workshop process to engage community members in talking about their community, and linking the stories to the discussions of redevelopment and resource development for communities. This work has been captured on the website, storymapping.org, which has also shared the stories of several other place-based projects from around the world.

Fourth Interlude

Reasons to Believe

Why do some people endure great sacrifices?

This is the story of my grandparents, Fernando and Emilia Sanchez.

When my grandfather arrived in Texas in 1944, he found himself, as many Mexican laborers did, Desenraizando la tierra. Clearing the Mesquite brush is perhaps one of the hardest jobs my grandfather ever did. My grandfather has spoken of the extreme heat that made is job nearly impossible.

Their workday started at seven in the morning and ended at ten at night. His leathery skin and calloused hands are evidence of the demanding nature of his work. His Patron, Rudolph Bell, was so impressed by Fernando's work that he asked Fernando to bring his family over from Mexico. He promised them housing and work on his ranch.

The Sanchez family arrived in Ed Couch, Texas, in 1945.

However, things were not so easy. When the Sanchez family arrived, there was no housing ready for them. My grandmother speaks of how for several nights the family had to sleep on a flat bed trailer. She speaks of how there was little defense against the cold mornings and the Sereno that would bring an unbearable chill to their bones.

My grandfather worked out in the fields for el Señor Bell seven days a week, from sunrise to sunset. My grandfather would even get his children to work in the fields to help finish the work faster.

For over twenty years, Mr. Bell compensated my grandfather with twenty-five dollars per week. My grandmother was paid two dollars per week for taking care of all the house chores and the cooking for the Bell family. The children were not paid for their services.

For over twenty years my grandparents saw their children grow up while they served el Señor Bell y su familia. My grandfather was completely devoted to his patron. After all, Mr. Bell had promised him two acres of his land, once he would have passed away.

When the Bell's fiftieth wedding anniversary occurred, my grandparents gathered as much money as they could and bought el Patrón y la Mamá the biggest floral wreath that was present at the Bell's fiftieth wedding anniversary celebration.

Rudolph Bell passed away in 1966. Shortly thereafter, the Sanchez family was ordered off their property by Mr. Bell's children.

Fernando attempted to make his case that Mr. Bell had promised him two acres on his ranch. However, the remaining Bell family would not honor Mr. Bell's promise.

The Sanchez family once again had to start from scratch. Fortunately, Fernando had invested in some land a quarter mile down the road. That's where they would settle down and start the rebuilding process, in the middle of a cotton field.

In 1975, Fernando retired after working another nine years for another Anglo farmer.

I've often wondered why Fernando and Emilia sacrificed so much of their lives by working out in the fields.

I think I now know why.

Muchas gracias por su gran sacrificio.

Su nieto, Ernesto Ayala.

Sacrificios
—Ernesto Ayala

© 2000 Ernesto Ayala. Images and text all rights reserved.

Although we have been at this work for fifteen years, and traveled around the world teaching and sharing our methods, I have only had a couple of opportunities to return to my home state of Texas to teach our process. In 2000, we received a significant grant from the W.K.K. Kellogg Foundation to assist with a program called Managing Information In Rural America. The program had the laudable goal of supporting grassroots community activists in designing and implementing technology-centered community development plans in a group of twenty-four pilot projects around the rural United States.

As luck would have it, one of the projects took us down to the Rio Grande Valley in far South Texas to assist an organization called the Llano Grande Center. This organization, like many community groups, was primarily focused on the youth and education. They had tremendous programs in media, a radio station, youth advocacy, and college preparation. The college prep program was so successful that they were getting twenty percent of their seniors into out-of-state colleges including Ivy League and West Coast schools. Keeping in mind that the average family income was under $10,000/year and eighty percent of the parents did not have high school-level educations, this was an extraordinary task.

In fact, at one point, there were so many Ed Couch students at the prestigious Brown University in Rhode Island, that they formed their own student group. More impressively, many of these students were coming back to teach and mentor their younger brothers, sisters, cousins and friends. One of these students was Ernesto Ayala, and as he shared the tale of his grandparent's life of labor and sacrifice, he captured a simple, but profound story.

Having grown up in Texas to parents who spent a large amount of time organizing Latino laborers into unions and working to defend and expand the civil rights of the disenfranchised throughout the South, I knew the Sanchez family story. And I knew the necessity of honoring their sacrifices and struggle for dignity.

In these stories, we look at our own life, our own values, and priorities. When we share them, we embrace history, even as we shape our shared future.

I can not imagine a more important role for our work.

11 Making Community

A Conversation with Thenmozhi Soundararajan

"Until lions have their own historians, tales of the hunt shall ever glorify the hunter."

—Ghanian Proverb

Thenmozhi Soundararajan is a filmmaker, singer, and grassroots media organizer. As a second generation Tamil Dalit/Untouchable woman, she strives to connect grassroots organizers in developing countries with media resources that can widen their base of resistance. From 1999-2001, she was the director and founder of the Center for Digital Storytelling's National Community Programs in which she developed the framework for community-based digital storytelling. In that capacity she has worked with over 200 communities around the country to develop new media practices for their work. Further, she is in residence at the MIT Center for Reflective Community Practice, writing about her experiences with community-based digital storytelling. She is also a 2001-2002 Eureka foundation fellow. Thenmozhi has also been featured by Utne Reader as one of the Top 30 Visionaries Under 30. Currently, she is co-founder and executive director of Third World Majority (TWM).

Joe Lambert: How did you become involved in digital storytelling?

Thenmozhi Soundararajan: I became involved with CDS in 1999 when I approached you and Nina after an open house about the possibility of being in residency at the Center or a possible internship. I was interested in addressing the ways to meld political film making, or facilitative film making, with an intentional organizing strategy. I did not have a fixed idea of what that would look like, it was a general value that I wanted to explore in the production process. I believed there was something urgent about this understanding and developing this practice in the new media realm was necessity not a choice.

One of the great strengths of CDS is that you were very flexible in allowing the space for my experimentation to occur, and the openness for theory to develop from the field. As I became involved in touring and teaching workshops, we would go out, return, discuss, and reflect back on our experiences. This would allow us to become honest and accountable as a group and as a program about all of our methods.

The time that I was CDS' Community Programs Director was a critical time for me. Very few young people get the opportunity to be so quickly immersed in all the aspects of a given methodology, from the tutorials, to the story circle, to the production supervision.

JL: You approached that responsibility with a background in Third World film-making. What experience did you bring into the practice of digital storytelling from your academic work and your experience as a filmmaker?

TS: I have been involved as an artist and an organizer in an ongoing process of defining a theory for facilitative media that is informed by third cinema for over five years now. As a movement, Third World Cinema emphasizes using film and video as means of connecting other struggles for self-determination within the community. The idea is that film as a production entity is subject to the same values that are present and inherent in the movement in which you are participating. So where in mainstream media they operate with a hierarchy of director and crew operating separate from the community they are documenting, the popular Third World filmmaker would organize production based on non-hierarchal systems of accountability in collaboration with the community.

© 1998 Thenmozhi Soundararajan.

I also wanted to look at the notion of skills transfer in doing media and documentary work. If you look at the way anthropology or media ethnography works, you have a skilled professional from outside the community documenting the people's lives and stories. When production is complete, and the work is distributed, the audience may have a larger exposure to the issues within this community, but there is little or no transfer of capital or skills. Conceivably, the filmmaker is provided access to the financial support for future projects, greater access to markets, and awareness of opportunities. But the community, in the long run, does not receive these benefits. Even when some degree of training or skills transfer takes place, there is often little thought about how the work can be made sustainable.

And it would be harmful enough if this was how most disenfranchised communities experienced filmmaking, but in many of the places and with people with whom I work, there is a long history of trauma with the camera and in general with technology. So for my practice, and for the theory we are developing to inform this practice, we also need methods to create a safe space for members of the community to discuss these issues.

JL: When you say a long history of trauma, to what are you referring?

TS: Whether it is the Internet or the camera, or the computers and how we structure them, all of these technologies have particular legacies of colonialism, and military and police intervention. For example, the Internet, the original ARPA-net, was a direct result of a scientific and military collaboration to develop a communications system for times of military crisis in the 1970's. While part of this was related to Cold War concerns, it was also occurring in the backdrop of counter-intelligence and repression within many of the communities of color in the U.S. If you look at film and video, you just have to look at the role mainstream media plays in our communities. The images that are portrayed create negative stereotypes, but more insidiously, they promote passivity and powerlessness. In the longer historical sense, as the cultural critic Coco Fusco has commented, the camera was used for ethnography and anthropology as the first line of colonial engagement with Native populations. This trauma is remembered by people, even as it is reinforced today by the fact that almost every part of our lives are now under surveillance with video cameras. As a result it is a double-edged sword when you take on the use of media technologies in a grassroots context.

JL: Part of your awareness of these issues comes from your own political experience and your own cultural background and nationality. You have worked in the area of Dalit culture, the issues of Indian and South Asian culture? Can you talk about how this affected your own work as a filmmaker and cultural activist?

TS: One of the reasons why I was so insistent about learning film and video technique is that many times people in different political contexts make media work the last priority. I am a second generation US citizen, from the Tamil Dalit people of India. We are at the very conservative counts at least 250 million people, almost as large as the population of the US. Yet very little is known about my culture and people, even in the context of South Asia. The reason why is that we exist as a community that has been oppressed for thousands of years. In India, you do not hear much about us because the media is controlled by the Brahmin press. Our voices and the media that has been distributed has come out through much hard-won grassroots infiltrations.

For us to take our struggle to the next level we need to produce our own media. We need to be the ones that define what our own images are like, because all throughout our history other people were defining who we were. We were given the name, Untouchables, by the Hindus, and given the name "Scheduled Castes" by the British. Who our Gods are, what our values are, and what defines our cultural heritage in their eyes has always been negative.

Much of our building a base of resistance included both the fight to reclaim our civil rights, like in the U.S., but also to reclaim our culture. This is why I am so drawn to that Malcolm X quote, "Culture is our ultimate weapon." Because once we take back our stories, cultures and values within our communities or nations, no matter what they do to you, they can't take back that essential sense of beauty that is you, and that is always your own. Fighting for your culture is fighting for your dignity. Perhaps more than ever in the current context of globalization and the globalization of culture based on the U.S. media's depiction of the world, we have to battle for cultural and political self-determination.

JL: Part of your perspectives grow from a perspective of a Third World youth, and the issues of young people vitalizing the current anti-globalization movement. Can you talk about your perspective as a youth activist?

TS: Young people have always been a part of movements. I want to resist the segmentation of a youth sector of the movement as being somehow exceptional. There is a perception, among funders for example, that youth deserve special support as long as they are youth. But as soon as they emerge as adults, the efforts to educate, expand their social consciousness, and connect them to their larger communities is somehow less important.

In the context of our media work, in the late nineties, we had the discussion of the "Digital Divide" in our schools and questions of access for youth to new technologies in our communities. It was approached that the computer was going to be a way of salvation, but without a thoughtful consideration of the ways that you integrate technology as part of the struggle to address the issues that are the bread-and-butter issues like welfare reform, rent control, police brutality etc., and what is the best way to build and support the cultures within the community.

People were training community folks, especially in our schools and community technology environments, without an intentional curriculum and practice for how training should be adapted to a specific community practice. In effect there was a lot of damage done, and it put our youth and other members of our communities back into the abusive relationship to technology that mirrored the historical legacies of transgressions against these communities.

I feel like that is one of the areas that CDS Community Programs, and now in my work with Third World Majority, fill a valuable space of linking the values of the movement to the way you teach these technologies. That's why we choose the teachers that we do. That is why we show the stories that we show. We are very conscious about how we relate with each other, with ourselves, and with the technology.

One of the things that was really interesting was that, in the anti-globalization movement, there was the role of the independent media centers in providing alternative media coverage of the events of Seattle and beyond. We knew that we would not get that positive of mainstream coverage, so we said, "let's compile all the resources, all the knowledge and let's set up our own independent media networks." This model of movement-oriented, independent media networks has spread to over 20 countries around the world. Anytime there is a particular political flare-up or crisis situation, within a couple of days there is an independent media center that brings journalists and provides equipment to cover the story. Their approach is to broadcast the voices of the people involved in those situations. I think that it has been very threatening to the mainstream media because many people are now going to these alternative news resources as their main source of unmediated news.

At the same time, the alternative media movement also has to address our own production standards, while our grassroots low-tech image was helpful in initially building trust with many communities. There is a larger struggle within the movement to incorporate high production values to help gain credibility with a broader audience. That is the next step of our work.

JL: You talked about the values of community digital storytelling, can you talk what you think some of those values are?

TS: The main focus of our organizing strategy is how community folks can best learn the story and technical skills and make the program they create around their own needs self-sustainable. We have a facilitative training process, similar to the CDS structure, where there is a teacher and an assistant teacher, but we also make sure there is a community teacher that we are collaborating with whose community wisdom is given equal weight to the "technical" knowledge of the other trainers present.

Another value we practice at TWM is teaching with curriculum that comes from the community we are working with. There are two parts to why we follow this concept. First, technology curriculum at schools and educational institutions has caused an incredible trauma within our communities because the textbooks, the software, and the hardware, are not are not built with the history and cultural context of our communities in mind. So when you are setting up a training environment, you have to be really deliberate about what images, sounds, and effects are presented, because people are already expecting to be shut down. So it is really important to have curriculum that comes from our communities' perspective—that speaks to our own ideas and the value systems that are embedded in the way we tell stories.

Secondly, stories are extremely different from community to community, from culture to culture, because they represent a collective wisdom drawn from implicit values not easily accessed at first glance. As we were talking about, some communities value non-resolution in story. In Western communities, everything is always about resolution. But in many non-western communities there is not the same insistence that the story has a definitive moral lesson or central insight. Accepting ambiguity is part of the wisdom of their culture. This sense of how stories are told is a vital connection to their entire approach to language and culture.

JL: Tell me about your new organization, Third World Majority?

TS: Third World Majority is a young women of color, political new media training center dedicated to global justice. As a collective, our mission is to develop new media practices for radical social change that challenge the notion that a media organization cannot also do grassroots political organizing. Our programs explore the interrelated nature of politicized new media production that includes digital video, the web, graphic design, sound engineering, and animation. Through our efforts and collaborations with other organizations, we support organizing in real, representational, and virtual worlds.

When we started TWM we had very few answers but lots of questions. Why do we feel uncomfortable around technology? Why is the culture of training and learning of technology so inaccessible? Why are all the techies we know white, alpha-male assholes? Why are media labs, tech centers, and public access stations so often empty not used by communities of color, and why is the damn media democracy movement so white?

Clearly the first big step for our work was reframing a lot of approaches to technology in the context of understanding its military and colonial legacy, but then we really needed to put our proactive vision out next. We recognized first and foremost that since media spaces were places associated with past and current drama (including a host of service-oriented techies who have only barely evolved from their well-meaning anthropological missionary counterparts from colonial times) that whatever we did in TWM meant that we could not build a physical lab for people to come into. Creating a technology space and then expecting to become a "community center" is a ridiculous concept. There is nothing inherently built into a computer that engenders community building (in fact it is exactly the opposite). So with our first seed-grant we bought a seven-station portable G4 laptop lab similar to the one I worked with at CDS. With the laptops, we could train in spaces that communities already felt at home with, so we taught around the country in barns, churches, community centers, schools, and people's homes. With the technology being both portable and rather small, folks were able to focus on the cultural products they were translating and reshaping into a digital medium rather than stress about the technology itself. It also prioritized for us the primacy of the community and the use of technology as tool, and just a tool.

The other aspect of our teaching process we needed to tackle was how to unpack the assumptions around the coded-boy's club nature around technology. As young women of color who had been early adapters of web and video technologies for the movements that we had been part of, we had all faced being shut out of labs, being condescended to by other techies, and learning the tools on curriculum that, at best, was not relevant, or at worst, was horribly offensive. We also realized that as working-class young women of color in a racist, sexist, classist society, our leadership and vision for our communities is always silenced (inside and outside of lab spaces).

So we began to rebuild the matriarchy, literally. We prioritized the leadership of young women of color as our trainers, organizers, and tech support. When folks come to one of our trainings, one of the standard lines we hear is "Wow, I never have seen so many young women, let alone young women of color know what they are doing around so many computers!" "Yeah," I say, "and we even know how to program our own VCRs!" It's funny how so simple a shift of *who* is teaching is not a simple thing at all. Because, while it literally changes the face of who is training, the other thing that happens is that I think relationships built within this context are also different. And while this is not to repeat stereotypes of gender binaries, but as an organization we are working towards modeling collective, intentional, nurturing models of leadership.

Finally, I think as young women, we assert and recognize the leadership women have had for a long time in our communities from mother to daughter, to nurture the passing on of our stories, culture, and traditions. This is an extremely important role young women continue to play, and we believe it is vital to recontextualize our work as not just technology trainings but as spaces of our cultural resistance.

JL: Can you tell some stories about some of the contexts in which you have been doing your work?

TS: What comes to mind is the large project we just completed in conjunction with the Active Element Foundation, an organization that builds relationships between grassroots networks among youth organizers and artists, and hooks them up with funding sources and retreat with sixteen of their youth groups from around the country, as a state-of-the-movement gathering. The funding came at the last moment, and we had two weeks to find a place, locate the equipment, book the tickets, and organize the logistics for the event. But we did it and it was one of the most amazing experiences I have ever been a part of.

At this workshop, much of the politics were explicit and the focus on using the workshop for a reflection on the movement was a top priority. Many times when people come to a film and video workshop, or even in the short history of digital storytelling workshops, they think of it as a training opportunity. We said, yes, the training and skills transfer, and producing a finished story are all important, but the collaboration and the story sharing was critical. We wanted to see the relationships build across movements, across issues, and between agencies, so we prioritized our time to insure that this could happen.

We used the workshop to provide a model for resistance culture in several ways. While we were teaching film and video, and showing great examples of digital stories, we also had people share chants, and songs from the different movements from around the country. People could then walk away knowing the issues of the struggles, but also know the values and the songs people sing to share and celebrate their resistance. We created a place where people wanted to share, stay up for late night cyphers (music/performance parties), in what was essentially, a week long cultural festival.

Then when we had the Saturday night public event, we had people go up and perform and do spoken word, introduce their pieces, and share songs. It was one of best weekends of my life, and several people came up and said that it had been one of their best weekends, because they had never had that space open for them, a space where hope was alive. We de-value the ways that culture creates political power. That is the biggest thing that we sometimes forget is that culture is our hope, and if we lose it, we lose a lot of what is viable to shape the direction of our future.

JL: How were the teachers selected?

TS: We selected teachers that had organizing experience–that was the first priority. Secondarily, we had people with the digital storytelling technical skills. In most of our workshops, we are constantly developing the production skills in seasoned community organizers from our collaborating communities, so that those skills will remain in the community.

JL: What do you think is transformative for the participants in the digital story-telling process?

TS: So much of how we structure the workshop is influenced by popular education teaching methods. Popular education begins where people are, and in our workshops we begin with the wisdom people hold within themselves and in their stories. So for me the most transforming part of the workshop is always the story circle. The sacred and safe space offered within a story circle allows people to build empathy with the stories and each other, even when those issues are divisive and controversial.

Many times when you bring people from contrary positions in any other context around the world, they are going to come out against each other from what they believe is their objective position on the issues. But within the story circle you reframe their relationship where they are both storyteller and listener.

When you inscribe two people like that within the same narrative, that inscription builds bonds of solidarity, and builds relationships in ways that would not have happened before.

In the Active Element workshop we had youth from communities like the Bay Area, New York, Cincinnati, Selma, and Milwaukee. We also had folks from urban and rural contexts. There was this one particular moment, where one of the students, whose name was "Life," was talking about the Cincinnati riots. He described the history of racism and segregation in Cincinnati. He said when that stuff went on, and sixteen people were killed, "You knew it was coming, knew it would happen, and it took us three minutes to take back a city, a city that had been taken away from us all the way along. And imagine," he said, "imagine if we were developed. Imagine if we had each other's backs. If we were a movement, how little it would take to recreate the world in the way that we want." And people in the group said, "Yeah, imagine that, and imagine that, etc."

There were other youth from a group called Young Women United from Albuquerque that created this amazing piece about the violence that young women of color face in their homes, schools, and neighborhoods. The way they told the digital story was circular, and they all talked about what it was like to be young women of color facing the interlocking systems of oppression, but also how they resist together, their voices told in a round only doubled their story's power. And everyone was like, "Damn, that's it." All the participants fed off of the love and hope they gave each other."

There was this enormous release within the workshop because of the level of frustration that most of us feel in grappling with all the issues within our communities. The problems with the accountability of institutions in our community; the education system, the lack of economic sustainability, the criminal justice system, gentrification, environmental justice... I mean the list goes on and on. At the same time, these young people are also involved in providing key leadership, connecting people, and mobilizing the resistance needed in their communities. So it was really powerful when the links were made in that story circle. And the links that were made from that excellent beginning were deepened throughout the rest of the workshop process.

If you are teaching the workshop with an intentionality around relationships and community building, you facilitate both for narrative and for relationships. It is a very subtle process in which that can happen.

JL: When you are doing a workshop, such as when we were working with one of the MIRA gatherings, there are subtleties that have to do with editorial decisions, leadership in collaborations, who remains voiceless in the collaboration, etc. Many times you can foresee the problems because you recognize the class, racial, or gender privileged attitudes of certain people in the collaborations, other times it is the subtleties of individual psychology.

Are these the subtleties you are addressing?

TS: These are all things that you would identify as a facilitator. Who is speaking in the room? Who is not speaking in the room? It also goes back further to the question of what license you are being given as a facilitator. If you have been asked to address issues of mediation and coalition building and you know there are difficult issues among the participants. One of the things I do, is show stories that would get to the issues even before the story circle. For example, if there are racial issues within a coalition, there are a set of stories that speak to different aspects of race relations from different contexts. So you set the stage for that process at the beginning when you are sharing and showing examples. So that by the mutual critiquing of the stories, it prepares people to address the issues in the story circle, and you can pull from references in the lecture.

Beyond facilitating to make sure that a discussion is not dominated by one particular view, the use of a team of facilitators also helps in that if the team has a unified approach, then you can decide who might be best to have specific discussions with a particular participant or group of participants.

JL: This means having the ability to customize the relationship with the participants with the strengths of each facilitator.

TS: Because of the "power" that people invest in teachers, you have an ability to act as a neutral force to address contradictions or issues that may arise. For example, in the MIRA project in Taos, there was a woman who spoke of her frustration with the Anglo establishment. The story she told was quite eloquent but she kept putting her piece down. At the same time there was an Anglo in the group who was expressing to her that he felt her piece was negative. In this context, as the teacher, I could extend out an alliance between these two, by suggesting to the Anglo that while it is very hard to hear criticism, it is important and necessary to be open to understanding the impacts of privilege. I could then also tell the woman that it is never negative to speak the truth about your resistance. It is the recognition that only through listening and building alliances can the struggle move forward.

This sort of intervention can bring down the heat inside the room, but with an effective team of teachers, they can have additional conversations with people to go into greater depth around contentious issues raised in the story circle during the rest of the workshop.

To sustain this, you need to have consistent discussion between teachers to make sure you are aware of the group dynamic.

JL: You spoke before about the legacy of a colonial model in the way people relate to technology. Can you talk about how that manifests?

TS: To be totally honest, I think people lie. I think people lie to folks who bring technology into their community because they do not trust these people, and so they provide a surface of their perspective, but don't really get down to their real feelings and stories. That is why it is so important to have facilitators that participants recognize as being from their community. As in, if you were working with Queer folks, having a Queer facilitator, or someone who is of a Native American background in the Native American context.

I think the other manifestation is about ownership. From the very beginning it should be clear what will happen with the stories and the images and material that are captured. Who will see the work and under what contexts? Because owning your wisdom and owning your images is something that was and continues to be taken away from many of these communities. So in a process like this, where you are trying to help people re-take control over the way their story is told as part of building their leadership, this needs to be explicit in the group discussions.

In the context of our program with Circle of Voices, a California Native digital storytelling project, we honored the sacred space of this gathering. What was discussed during the workshop was not to be discussed outside the workshop.

Also, all of the material was removed from the machines after the workshop. Also, the participants had personal copies of their stories, but we did not keep secondary back-ups. Finally, the material gets to be defined and used by the communities first.

JL: Part of what I was asking is do you see an inherent issue about computing machines, and their design, and their relation to historical cultural attitudes and contradictions? In other words, is there an inherent contradiction between the general computing culture and doing empowerment and cultural work?

TS: I would break it down in a couple of ways. As I mentioned, there is the lack of trust within communities of people who have, in the last couple of decades, been offering computers in these various communities. In regards to the computers themselves, I think it is important to remember how toxic computer manufacturing is, and to keep in mind who builds these computers. Whether it is in the Third World or in the U.S., it is mainly women who are vulnerable to both the repressive labor practices and the unregulated toxic exposure they face in these high-tech sweatshops. The computer designers and the computer engineers who design these fancy machines are not thinking much at all about the human cost of the manufacture. While computers are promoted as a green industry, they are in fact quite stained with blood.

I also think that the individualism of computer design is a reflection of the Western heritage. It is part of the legacy of consumerism where there is an expectation that people will use their technical devices in the privacy of their homes, alienating and separating people from each other. I think if you look at communities in the Global South, where technology applications have been approached with a different perspective, the emphasis is on communal use, on ways that people share the resource and maximize the productivity for the community's benefit. Now, in this culture, the computer is built for a single user, but it would be so much nicer if you had ways that multiple users could design and integrate their work together in a relationship context.

This extends even to the color palettes and design motifs of the computer world. There is little sensitivity to different ways of seeing between cultures. Of course, this is a reflection of who can currently afford the machines, but it also a particularly color—and culture—blind attitude that is particularly profound with the computer industry.

When you are teaching digital storytelling, you are quite aware that the software and hardware are both built in a very real, coded "boy" culture. And maybe more specifically, coded "boy-loser" culture. So much about how learning is transferred isn't collaborative. It is about one-upmanship, about "Oh, I have this, you don't. Oh, let me show you this thing." It is very much about competition, and is antithetical to collaboration. This reflects a dominant culture male attitude, but it also reflects privilege: who has time or money to spend days keeping up with all of the cool new gadgets, latest websites, and hot software.

So now most people coming to any technical training, including the digital storytelling workshop, don't feel they can relate to this world because the whole technology environment has been designed to serve this narcissistic boy culture, who were in a position to be the early adapters and designers of this technology because of their privilege.

All of that said, the reason I am still doing the work relates to my attitude about literacy. In the short term, the way technology is set up is not particularly good for our people and communities. We are talking about maybe the legacy of this particular evolution in the culture of personal computing will be with us for the next fifty to sixty years. This makes it a critical time for us to advocate change in the very infrastructure of these technology systems within our communities, and radicalize what it means for us to be global citizens. For us to become architects of the change in our understanding and use of technology, as opposed to compliant consumers, we need to be engaged as much as the dominant culture.

I think the community digital storytelling workshop is a really good introduction to this dialogue. It is a safe place where we can say, "Ugh, we have to put up with this technology. It is necessary for us to engage, but we are engaged with an exit strategy in mind." If you fail to present this value system to people you are introducing to the computing world, then you are only perpetuating the attitude of inferiority and disengaged compliance toward adopting technology among oppressed communities. This in turn leads to the continuation of hostile mistrust, if not complete rejection, of those technologies. The same dynamics get played over and over again.

JL: Where do you think your work is going?

TS: I feel like story is at the core of all my work. It is what actually gets people beyond the technology, after the "ooo and ah" of the shiny expensive equipment, the thing that stays is the story. Story is the critical connection between personal subjective experience and larger political action, between individual and collective action. And for me I am still exploring how magical that discovery can be for individuals and their communities.

There is a way I want to see the movement grow where ultimately each community agency is its own hub of experience. They would use the stories not just for external communications and coalition building, but as a way that they maintain their history, their story, within the values and parameters that define who they are. They can use it to access past moments to inform current struggles.

For example, in the "Joe Gotta Go" campaign (The recent Selma, Alabama mayoral contest where a white mayor, who had served from the days of his opposition to civil rights in the 1960s, was defeated and replaced by their first African American mayor), we did the piece, *Someone Died for Me*. It was an incredible externalization of how they do the work and why they do that work, at a critical moment in the campaign. They had been trying to get Joe Smitherman out of office for thirty-seven years, and the struggle had truly come to a head in the summer of 2000. I had been assisting them with mainstream media work, trying to call attention to Selma through a series of op-ed pieces, press releases, and radio spots when the idea came of trying to do a digital story/music video based on an important song in Selma Civil Rights history that spoke of the tremendous sacrifices people had made to get the right to vote. They wanted to use this song to help people link the past struggle to that of the current voter fraud, and all the blocks the white establishment had put in front of the black community's disenfranchisement.

When we finally finished the digital story, we were in this big church, and the movie was going to be shown, actor, Sean Penn, and Black Panther activist, Geronimo Pratt, were there, and the biggest moment was not when the famous people spoke, but when the community saw those pictures. For people outside the South like myself, the pictures we used have an important historical interest, but for folks from Selma, the people in those pictures were their aunts, their uncles, their grandfathers, their grandmothers, friends, and other loved ones who had personally been willing to give their life to be free—and some did lose their lives. People were crying, people were moved, and I was truly humbled.

You cannot underestimate what we can do when we are fully connected to our culture and values. Three or four days later, because of their collective will and struggle, they won that campaign.

JL: That is a wonderful example. Whether or not the film becomes part of the legacy of Selma's struggle, or was just used for that particular moment, it is an incredible new gift to offer communities in these historical moments the tools to capture the emotions and perspectives of a struggle.

TS: It was incredibly important that it be seen, that it was three young women of color who co-directed this piece, with the other collaborators being another woman from Selma and a woman from Mali. It wasn't that the piece had been created by someone Sean Penn had brought from Hollywood, it was home-grown by people that generally would not have access, or be recognized for speaking up, let alone pick up a camera! I mean, people *still* talk about it.

JL: Regarding the Internet, there is a protocol about honoring the sacredness of the story circle, and we have not found an easy way to publish or broadcast the material that sustains those protocols. We do not have a mechanism via the Internet that invites people to be part of the experience, but how can we gauge the potential of an anonymous audience, and if it has developed the maturity or sensitivity that would allow them to understand the author's intent? An anonymous audience may not be able to contextualize the risks and vulnerability the authors of some of these pieces have taken. You have been approaching these issues, so what are your thoughts?

TS: All of us have been struggling with what is the most effective way to distribute these pieces. Traditionally, when you created media, as independent media artists or as documentarians, your option for distribution was film festivals, public access TV, or targeted direct-to-video distribution to homes. Now we can use the web and broadband connections to reach a larger but narrower audience. In most of these situations you cannot control the parameters of the audience and how the work is contextualized, which is important if the intention of the showing of the piece is to build community or encourage more stories.

JL: The problem for me is that broadcast, the notion of endless media that is pumped in and around our lives, is an inherently horrible cultural practice. While most media is filtered by our sense of interest and engagement, it is to one degree or another diminished by the noise of media ubiquity. We, as has been said, are a nation of neurotic channel surfers.

This creates an impossible system of valuation, because none of it feels relevant. We need circles of consideration–communities of context that provide stories, or suggest stories, that through their familiar relation to us, their knowledge of our life path and interest, can enlighten us. This is the idea of word of mouth. People say, "This story is relevant. You should see it," or put another way, "See it in this context, because I think it is relevant to you." I would much prefer seeing these stories travel by email, or locked behind a password and encryption system, for which a community shares a key.

So part of our work is imagining beyond broadcast, and defining the terms of the ways that these authentic stories find their way to media environments. We are proud of our work with BBC-Wales because we think we have instilled a sense of seriousness, of caution, or sensitivity into the media professionals carrying out these community processes.

TS: I agree that we need these considerations. But what I would like to see is these dialogues not just be between entities of the Global North, or by experts coming from the North to "educate" the South, but to see exchanges promoted between representatives of one cultural practice in the South to another culture or community in the Global South. Can you imagine a training and discourse on digital storytelling between our friends in Mali and the Dalit communities in India? The problem is that funders do not see this as a necessity. It is very easy, relatively speaking, to have someone from the First World get funded to go south, have their transformative experience, and at the same time do a little to help the natives. It is almost impossible for experts in the South to get that same level of funding.

In terms of this work being conducted internationally, it is very important that the values and approaches of the teachers get examined, but also look at who is teaching, and who is in the room. You have a few days to work with people, and people will definitely censor themselves based on the sense they are among people, that the leadership of the workshop would validate and defend their perspectives.

Going back to distribution, what we have been advocating for is looking at community-based venues of distribution as a component of community building. We think community curation is the preferable option over external events, like film festivals. Partly because in the context of community curation, the digital story can be produced with a whole series of other community cultural practices including, song, dance, and spoken word, that sets the story in the larger framework.

We need to re-program our communities to connect with these community story venues, to make choices about whether to spend all their dollars on mainstream media or come see films about people they know, and through which they recognize their own story.

Because from the making, sharing, and screening of these pieces we are not just creating alternatives to the mainstream. We are creating our own lasting institutions, the beauty of which we discover story by story; community to community.

12 The Change Within

A Conversation with Caleb Paull

"While in our daily lives we move between worlds in which our selves are different and even contradictory, in the authoring of self we make choices and negotiate between these selves that exist in different contexts and social worlds. From the reflective space of constructing story, in responding to and addressing the social worlds, roles, and codes of our lives, we can begin to form a sense of self-control, and a basis for self-direction."

Excerpt from *Self-Perceptions and Social Connections*
—Caleb Paull, ©2002 All Rights Reserved.

Doctor Caleb Paull, Ed.D, is a recent doctoral graduate of the University of California, Berkeley, School of Education. His dissertation, *Self-Perceptions and Social Connections: Empowerment through Digital Storytelling in Adult Education*, connected digital storytelling to discussion of educational philosophy, and the applications of the process in an educational setting. Caleb has been an educator for 10 years, having worked as a writing and composition teacher in his native New York City and in the Bay Area. From 1999-2001, he served as the Education Program Director of the Center for Digital Storytelling. He currently lives in Chicago, Illinois where he works as a coordinator in Roosevelt University's Teacher Quality Enhancement Project.

Joe Lambert: How did you get involved in digital storytelling?

Caleb Paull: I became involved in digital storytelling through my graduate advisor at the School of Education in UC Berkeley, Glynda Hull. She had taken a workshop with other teachers in a writing program at Berkeley, and she had produced a piece about her childhood and her parents. In my visits with her every week, I would usually arrive and tell her I wanted to drop out of graduate school. On one of those visits she said to me, "Oh, I have to show you this thing that I made," and she tried to describe how she used photographs and she'd used music and made some kind of movie. I didn't really know what she was talking about. She put the videotape in the VCR and showed me her movie. I said, "Wow, that's amazing." I knew that was something I really want to do.

In high school, I ran a Public Access cable television show. I had a bit of experience in television and video at Brown University and after my work at Brown, but I had never worked with computer video editing. Video production had always been extremely difficult, and I relied on institutions that had huge expensive machines to do analog video editing. And Glynda said "Oh no, I did it all on the computer, in a few days." I thought if I could work that into my studies that it would be a reason to actually stay in graduate school.

As I recall, I was taking a course at the time called Curriculum Studies and I thought this could be really interesting in terms of classroom uses and uses for teachers and their own professional development. So I decided to write a paper on the history of technology in the classroom. What I found was that, historically, different technologies had been pushed into the classroom from above rather than in response to teachers' desires or needs. Consequently there was a history of resistance to technology by teachers, as technology often interfered with their classroom goals. The headaches of learning these new technologies and troubleshooting technical problems simply weren't worth it. Teachers, for the most part, have not felt comfortable with using technology themselves, which was reflected in how they imagined implementing it in their curriculum. At the end of the paper, I took a look at new directions in educational technology, directions that might be more meaningful and valuable in terms of teachers' and students' goals. I put digital storytelling out there as one of those directions.

Around that time, I called you and you offered me some material you had been writing, and by a happy coincidence the next semester, the Center for Digital Storytelling moved into the College of Education in Berkeley and offered its first course.

I've always wanted to be a screenwriter and a director and now I'm a teacher– let's see if I can meld them all together. So I took your class and the rest is history.

JL: Let's talk about your first experience doing a digital story.

CP: Actually, if I could do it over again I would do it differently. When I did my first digital story, I used a piece of writing that I had written as part of my work with the New York City Writing Project. It was a narrative poem that about my experiences with my father's poker games when I was a child.

I don't remember if I felt very stuck with writing at the time, or perhaps I was so locked in to the type of writing that I was doing for graduate school that it was hard for me to create an original piece for the digital storytelling class. But this older piece worked, and I really wanted to use it to experiment visually with the writing. Particularly, when I think of my relationship with my father, it has always been based on enjoying films together.

JL: You have been interested in the writing process as a means at exploring identity for quite some time. Can you speak about how this background shaped your interest in digital storytelling?

CP: I'd been both teaching writing, and doing a lot of it on my own, and I saw writing as a way of reconstructing experience, and making sense and meaning out of one's life. But when the writing entered the realm of digital multimedia, I saw a number of new possibilities.

For example, on the story about my dad, when I wrote the piece, I was not thinking about our shared interest in film. The story was a nostalgic look back at childhood and the importance of being part of this community of men. When I was faced with the question, "How do I represent this visually?" I started to have new insights about other connections between me and my father. To represent poker visually, I brainstormed the idea of a number of films that have scenes of men smoking, of trails of smoke floating in the air. I realized that it's an additional level of meaning. And drawing on these movie clips could speak to my father as the audience, beyond the original text, communicating this shared bond around movies.

I remember these particular scenes that we saw together when I was a child. So it was also a recollection of our shared relationship. So beyond my original attempt to just reflect on my impressions on my father's male community, the digital story came to inform the way that I construct the basis of my relationship with my dad.

JL: Digital storytelling is about individual insight, but it is also meant to be an effective group process. What did you see in this first experience regarding the effect on the larger classroom?

CP: I was excited by the whole process. There was an unbelievable excitement about this approach, particularly within the context of school and graduate school. People were coming and going in the lab, working hard on their projects. They would share what they were doing, and I would show them pieces of my work. And we give each other super-positive feedback, and it was genuine.

I've been in classes where the norm is saying something positive, just before you tear them apart. But in the digital storytelling class, we were all trying to tell stories that were important to us, and we all faced the challenge of working creatively with unfamiliar tools, so there was a lot of leaning on one another, and mutual support.

Also I was older than many of the other students, and at a different point in thinking about my own identity. I saw undergraduates approaching telling their digital story in a somewhat defensive way. It was as if they were saying, "Okay I really don't want this to be that much about me. I'm not that comfortable with me, so I'm going to make it humorous or offensive or shocking."

Having that time in the class together and seeing where different people were willing to go, what they were willing to share, the strides that they took from the beginning to the end, was very revealing. Whether the final story was a deeply personal story or not, I still came to know them better. We could listen more honestly to whatever story that was being shared.

JL: So as luck would have it, we were able to hire you and put you on the road with our training approach. Can you talk as an educator about the way you viewed the methods of our workshop practice?

CP: To be perfectly honest, it's a little bit hard to take myself back to before this massive amount of work I recently completed about digital storytelling, so let me speak about how I look at it now.

JL: Yes, your dissertation has run over your brain.

CP: The environment that I first experienced digital storytelling was a semester-long process. This is completely different than the CDS three-day workshop. At first, when I began to participate in the local workshops, both as someone creating a story, and someone assisting people, I thought "This is great." Three days: it's intense. It brought me back to teenage longings for these intense moments with people where people get to know each other. "Let me open myself up to you, and you open yourself up to me. It'll be great."

And the three-day workshop *is* great. People have no choice but to get to know each other, and trust each other, and to take chances. The immersion allows the participants to go much deeper into the process than if it were a classroom that met for two hours, once a week. You experience levels of exhaustion and epiphany that I think you might not otherwise attain.

At the same time, what came to be very frustrating was that it was such a short space of time, then it was over. The longer that I assisted in these workshops, and started leading them, the more I felt that there was such a powerful base that was built and then it was being left behind. In some cases, some of the people would take their experience to another level, and do something with it. This was true when they would have sufficient support there to help them to continue.

But in many cases this amazing experience happened, and a skill set was built. There was a big wonderful celebration. Then it's over, and the participants go back to work on Monday. That was very frustrating to me as a teacher—as an educator—and I imagine, in many ways, it was very frustrating to many of the other participants as well.

I would imagine a year after one of the workshops, many people feel like it is really cool that I have this CD or movie. I can always show it to people, and be proud of that and say, "I did this. This was great." But I don't feel that they could have fully explored how the whole process could have informed their personal or professional lives beyond the workshop.

JL: I agree with you. But the irony is that we have found that in principally servicing professionals, three days is an extraordinary luxury. To leave your job and immerse yourself in a focused creative process, even if it directly relates to training and professional development, happens once-a-year, once in five years, for most professionals. We would like to imagine that reflection is built into professional practice, but in difficult economic times, we do not think we can easily expand this program to more days. As for follow-up, and seeking ways to integrate these practices into the day-to-day work of professionals and enthusiasts alike, this is where we see the need for much more curriculum development.

In working with classroom teachers, and with other educators, what are some of the applications you can imagine for this process?

CP: As a starting point, I think there are a number of considerations in implementing digital storytelling in an educational context.

First, teachers are tired. Teaching is a tiring profession. It is very emotional. Teachers are also tired of technology, as I said before. Technology has been pushed into the schools from above for years upon years. And rarely with any thought about as to how it would really integrate into actual classroom practice, or what teachers actually wanted to do, or about how it impacts the relationships within a classroom that are so important. My experience with teachers coming into digital storytelling is that they assume it is yet another technology program they are being sold, and they have a healthy skepticism about it.

But the teachers I have worked with—they're very good at telling their stories. Very rarely do people ask for their stories, and so just the act of asking is very powerful. So when you start with a story circle, or sharing initial writing samples from exercises, and demonstrate that what you are really interested in is their story and not selling them a new toolbox, they take interest.

And just the act of sharing those stories is the single most important part of a professional development experience, because it's creating community and a reflection on practice.

In making digital stories, teachers are given a new way to be creative. Creative artistic expression, particularly in the context of work, is not very encouraged.

It is fun. It's not just, "I gotta write an article for this journal about being an English teacher, and teaching reading to third graders." It's what interests me, what excites me, and how I can bring it into the context of the classroom.

I can speak for myself, and I think for many teachers, the one thing that makes teaching such a wonderful profession is the vitality of the classroom. It's the voices of the classroom, and the images of the classroom. *And,* it's the energy of the classroom. In normal processes of talking about that classroom, researching that classroom, and sharing the story of that classroom with other teachers, you're usually relying on words to communicate what is really a daily multimedia experience.

I don't think the process of classroom inquiry–of the role it can play in our schools–has been fully explored. Teacher ethnography is about collecting the pieces, collecting the artifacts, having some question in mind, and based on the question gathering all these things, but not being sure what story they're going to hold. In the gathering of these things, the question gets reshaped and the story begins to form, and in the telling of the story new insights are discovered about the classroom and eventually avenues for new stories open up.

And that's what I've seen happen with the teachers I've worked with, where they're re-energized about their teaching, because they're taking themselves back into the classroom, and they're also expressing it in this way that they've never been able to. They too begin to discover ways in which they can make meaning out of these classroom experiences that they might not have thought of before. But they also discovered that they can produce something that brings a whole new audience into the discussion about what's important about teaching, and what's important about their classrooms, and what's acceptable to parents, and other teachers, and to the students in the classes.

JL: Story is a much more effective repository of data than many research methodologies that use data points as metrics. But how can we expand the use of story as a research and assessment tool for educators?

CP: I am exploring digital storytelling as an action research tool, an iterative tool where the points of reflection develop a professional portfolio. The idea is to return to your earlier story, again and again, in each iteration, and have that shape the research questions and artifact collection over many semesters or years. I think that it can be very powerful. It hasn't been done.

When teachers do this work and have a way of coming together around it, it goes beyond just individual reflection on one's own practice, and it develops a community of reflective professionals. It should be part of what teachers are doing anyway.

JL: Talk about your application of digital storytelling in adult education.

CP: My background is in adult education. I've always worked with populations and individuals who enter the classroom timidly and not feeling that they have a lot to contribute. So much of my experience of digital storytelling was people's sense of excitement and discovery about the stories that they could tell and how they could tell them.

I've done work with remedial writing, and so the struggle was that students would enter these classes being told that they were not good writers, and writing is not fun for them. They don't feel comfortable taking chances and exploring their own voice. The process of digital storytelling broadens the definition of writing. With multimedia authoring, the student does not feel they are creating something out of nothing. At anytime you can't think of a word, you can look for a picture, and maybe that picture will spark a word or sentence or a paragraph. When you've exhausted your images, you listen to music and it offers other possibilities.

That's a big part of what interested me in the first place. Let the students who don't feel that there are opportunities to tell their stories, and even when I try to give them opportunities to tell their stories it's a struggle, let's give them all the tools and permission possible.

One of my favorite experiences in working with CDS was my role in the Institute for the Future workshop collaborating on a story with three students from a, as they put it, "messed up" high school in East Oakland. Here were three students who felt that they weren't receiving any kind of education in school, who were in the midst of a larger group of kids at the workshop who had been given tremendous validation for their writing in their schools. These three felt "we can't write like them" and therefore didn't write anything at all for the first week. Because of this fear of, and struggle with, writing, they seemed to believe that they didn't have important stories to tell.

To be able to sit down with them and say you do have a story to tell, tell it! And to have them speak and be able to record it and have their editing process be, "Let's listen back to our voices and choose the pieces that seem most important." Well that is what you do in writing, but suddenly there's a new option. They would say, "Hey, can we use movies that we really like?' I would respond, "Yes you can." Then they go, "Oh cool, there's this movie with this great scene." As it turns out that scene really represents a lot of what they're telling in their story.

All those avenues for expression have validated my interest in digital storytelling. In addition, adults coming back into education are often seeking new definitions and new identities and seeking concrete changes. They're choosing to come to school for some sort of transformation. To have them go through this process where they can use all these tools to explore why they are here and what is important in their lives and tell that to themselves and others is really important and empowering.

JL: What are some of the other revelations that have occurred to you in your research and practice?

CP: In doing media work with students, I expected the process would engender self-empowerment. That had been my own experience and I would have been surprised if the students came out the process without it. What surprised me more was the sense of audience.

Our experience is that a movie is public. Our students had a sense of the public nature of the piece as they were creating it. They were thinking about how the piece could help or influence other people in the community. One person telling a story about immigration to the U.S., and the transition to life in this country, led to them thinking about how such a story could be a great help to others going through similar processes. I wasn't giving them that as a direction in their writing and producing the digital story. They were not instructed that the story had to serve a larger public purpose. I'd never seen that happen with writing. Unless I specifically made that part of the assignment in writing, students would assume the discourse was private, or with me as the teacher, or at most with the classroom.

But with digital storytelling, the public role of their writing became part of the process–to have a social consciousness of their work. It brings a community together. Their sense of empowerment was about not only taking control of their own experience, but it also let them feel that they could face anything and that they were better writers.

In addition, creating a digital story takes people into an intense writing revision process. A much more careful, critical reflection is required with the introduction of images and music: *Will these words fit these pictures, have I written too much, can the picture express something more effectively than my prose, or does my writing need to tell what is missing from the image?* And of course, the visual editing process is also filled with revision, trial and error, and discovery. A student looking for a picture can search through 300 pictures before they find the right one, but they will know it when they find it. And that's a powerful process of revision, of editing, and of trying to get it just right. I have barely begun to explore how to teach more traditional writing through the creation of digital stories as opposed to create digital stories out of writing. For example, pivotal moments, detailed writing, how to bring the reader into the moment–it all has a powerful potential.

13 When Silence Speaks

A Conversation with Amy Hill

Amy Hill is a video maker, public health consultant, and organizer with ten years of experience working in community and health settings to end violence and abuse. In collaboration with the newly formed Third World Majority, she has been coordinating Silence Speaks: Digital Storytelling for Healing, Resistance, and Violence Prevention, which provides violence survivors, witnesses, and prevention advocates with the opportunity to create short digital videos about their experiences.

Joe Lambert: How did you get involved in digital storytelling?

Amy Hill: I came to this work at a point of frustration with the limitations in the approaches to media education that I saw in the domestic violence prevention field. Most of this media work was formed around didactic classroom presentations and curriculums that did not speak to the actual experiences of the victims. When I found about digital storytelling, I thought that it would be an effective way to develop and incorporate visual media into community education and public awareness campaigns related to violence against women.

As I understood the arts therapy potential of digital storytelling, which was over my first several experiences in making digital stories, I came to see that digital storytelling could provide a transformative experience for victims of domestic violence.

JL: When did you first make a digital story?

AH: My first experience was with the Digital Clubhouse Network, which I found through the research and consulting I was doing for domestic violence agencies to identify interesting uses of technology for capacity building. They still underutilize technology and computers in general, so I was looking for an interesting way to engage them that wasn't as dry as introducing them to basic software applications. So I stumbled upon the DCN on the web, and spoke with them, and they put me in a workshop that was specifically for non-profits agencies.

The DCN methodology is a bit different from CDS. They had the participants teamed up with a young person that handled the production work on the computer. The participant wrote the script, brought the pictures, and provided direction for the edit of the movie.

What I took away from the Clubhouse experience was two key things. One is that in telling my own story about my own experience with violence I realized that we needed to have workshops dealing with those specific issues. My comfort level was not very high in dealing with the subject matter in the context of a larger, more generally focused environment. The second point was realizing the importance of directly empowering the participants in the use of the technology—to have them produce the pieces. My understanding of the strength of this approach came as I began working more with CDS.

JL: In your own experience, why do you think digital storytelling is useful as a reflective practice?

AH: There are a couple of things. From the perspective of working in the field of violence against women there is a fair amount of media that is presented in the guise of health education, and prevention, that end up as these canned, unrealistic scenarios. Most people in the field do not find that helpful. In having gone through the process myself, and having told my own story, and having coordinated a series of workshops with survivors and witnesses and people that do this work, there is a level of authenticity that comes through in the digital stories. It has a way of connecting other people. The digital story presents what a person that has been affected by violence has experienced in a way that the more dramatized, and canned approach does not.

Because I work with a number of domestic violence agencies, we end up working with staff members. In these agencies we have a great deal of discussion about how you draw the line between working directly with survivors and working with staff in setting up the workshops. What I have found is that the line is actually gray and blurry because a number of people that work in the field actually have some direct experience with violence in their own lives. Because staff members in these agencies understand there is such a great need for their services, they work a million hours for little money, what we found is that, across the field, they don't have much time to reflect back on how their own experience affects the works that they do. Nor do they have time to step back and look at their experience in a way that provides for their own cathartic transformation.

In working with people at different agencies it has been enormously powerful for them. It has been an amazing team building experience. And where we have brought together representatives from numerous agencies it has also been an effective cross-agency support building process. People have told stories across a broad spectrum of issues related to violence: from human rights work in Colombia, to a young man who works at Men Overcoming Violence who told a story about his own involvement in gangs, and how that experience informs his work as a youth guidance counselor. This spectrum of story allows people to make connections regarding the way different forms of violence are related.

JL: What do you see is unique to your approach to digital storytelling? As you moved toward a therapeutic practice, what sort of ethical and political questions did you have to address?

AH: Fortunately we have done enough workshops to have a body of work to begin to assess these issues in a way that I believe can make this process sustainable. As for the therapeutic benefit, the best way to express this is through an example from what someone said after participating in one of the workshops. A participant said that the workshop experience allowed him for the first time to have complete control over the telling of a story that related to a situation over which he had no control. So it was a way of reclaiming your own experience that allows you autonomy and agency in how you portray it back to the rest of world. That is a general feeling about the process and how it can be intensely cathartic.

People who participate in these workshops generally self-select. In other words, the workshop attracts people that have already gone through therapy and done some work with their issues, so this process takes them to a different level. It is one thing to sit with a therapist or in a group therapy session and just talk about their experience, but it is something all together different to put words to the experience, create a visual treatment of it, and incorporate music, and all the multimedia elements. It gives a person multiple levels of meaning to work with and describe the experience.

JL: What about the participant's sense of social agency? Do you think this shapes their sense of contributing to the struggle against violence?

AH: Yes, most people experience a radical change in the idea of what they are going to do with their story project, from when they first hear about the project, to when they arrive and are oriented for the workshop, and again it changes as they move toward producing their piece. As teachers, we make sure that their decision about how to use the piece is always completely up to the participant in terms of what context that they want to show it in.

As a testament to their commitment of it having an impact on the world, we have found that most people are quite comfortable with us using the pieces on the website, or compilation tapes, or different community settings, conferences, film festivals, etc. They see it as a way to showcase their work and to stimulate more community dialogue about the issues.

I can say that whenever I have presented the work, or from the Silence Speaks website, the response has been hugely supportive from the constellation of professionals dealing with violence.

JL: Even in our public workshops, people are willing to take risks with emotional material, and ordinarily they are prepared for the emotional impact of this work, but sometimes they are not. How do you address people's potential for going into crisis as part of the workshop experience?

AH: This is an important part of our learning from our work in the last two years. In addition to self-selection of participants, we make sure they understand that the workshop is not appropriate for someone currently in crisis or coming out of crisis situation. We make that clear in our materials and what we say to would-be participants or agencies representing participants. In addition we have worked with social workers with a history of working with groups to develop a self-assessment question for potential participants to think through whether or not they feel prepared to participate. The questions include: *Have you told the story before? What was your experience when you told the story? What kind of support do you think you might need in the context of the workshop or beyond?*

While we indicate that none of us are licensed therapists, we have a great deal of grassroots experience in the field. For example, I am certified as a rape crisis counselor.

We did a collaboration with San Francisco's Women Against Rape which has a writing program called Fearless Words, which works with survivors of sexual assault. For that program, one of the facilitators for the writing component was a social worker that had experience working with groups, and she was part of our project. She could be tapped to provide support if anyone needed.

In terms of curriculum adjustments, the biggest difference is that for the three-day workshop, we spend twice as much time on the story circle. We need to discuss more and process more, so we reduce the lecture and tutorial sections.

With workshops with women, or specifically women of color, we make sure the instructors are all women or women of color. This creates a safe space for people to participate and open up around issues.

JL: Do you have an intuitive assessment of how your experience in working in these therapeutic contexts might be relevant to other areas of the health professions?

AH: We feel that our work in digital storytelling links directly to the traditions of narrative therapy and art therapy, about which there is substantial research of its positive effects on recovery. Narrative therapy has addressed both the general power of re-writing the life story you carry with you, as well as the specific impact that the writing process has in reflection, and feedback in a therapeutic environment. Art therapy addresses creative expression in general.

JL: I had the experience early in our digital storytelling process of working with an incest survivor that was particularly poignant to me. I realized that for a survivor, going through the family album was a painful journey into a territory of denial that was represented in the snapshots of happy family gatherings. In the specific piece, there was a photo of a parent, the father in this case, who was the abuser, and the image captured in the body language of the child, and even the expression on her face, a sense of separation and distance. In working on her edits, the survivor was able to deconstruct that image, to call attention to details, and take control of the meaning of the image in a new way. And as she talked about her experience in the film, her voice added another layer of depth and complexity. It was enormously powerful.

AH: There is a wonderful book, *Home Movies and Other Necessary Fictions*, by Michelle Citron, a feminist filmmaker and theorist at the University of Chicago. She made a film in which she took home movies from her family and re-explored power dynamics in her family. It was her way of taking ownership in a production sense that had situated her as a child on the other side of the camera. So she twists this around and takes on the role, in this case, of her father, who was the one with the camera.

While she was a professional and had training to do this, digital storytelling is allowing anyone to use similar tools to explore a very similar process, to re-examine, reclaim and explore the aspects of their experience. In that sense, I think this is really groundbreaking.

There is also a way in which some of the modes of art therapy and narrative therapy can also be inappropriately clinical, and not very accessible in a community context. This can turn off many young people, and particularly women of color. As such, there is a little hesitancy on our part to align too closely with the therapeutic arena because we see what we are doing as more grassroots, and culturally relevant.

JL: In that sense it relates more to the notions of co-counseling and peer counseling movements that have tried to position themselves not as opposition to the professional medical priesthood, but as effective alternative for a large number of people. Are there other adaptations in your practice?

AH: In terms of comparing experiences, there are two key things in the past year. One, in the project with Women Against Rape, we met as a group for two hours for eight weeks prior to the three-day workshop. This allowed for the time to get to know each other and bond as a group, as well as develop scripts. I also did the storyboarding session in advance. We also had an art night where people did artwork, that people either did or did not use in their final pieces. Then everyone came into the workshop with a developed idea of their script as well as a fairly developed sense of the storyboard.

So what that experience showed me was that the three-day crash course by itself is not particularly appropriate for survivors. There is enough anxiety about the technology component alone, that it became much more gratifying to me, as well as the participants, to rationalize the larger commitment of time and resources.

The limitation is that this works for a local practice, but not one in which we are trying to work with people in communities outside the Bay Area. We cannot imagine being away for these extended periods, and it means we would have to trust our collaborators in another area to facilitate this whole portion of the experience.

The other learning experience we had was teaching a workshop with an organization in Arizona called Tuba City for Family Harmony with Navajo and Hopi Women. On the other end of the spectrum in terms of preparation, we were working with women who really could not come for three entire days because of jobs, childcare and transportation. So we rethought the workshop, and fortunately we had a small number of participants, so we were able to work one-on-one as couselors to develop stories. They recorded their script and did the editing, but we assisted with production, such as the Photoshop process.

The Tuba City workshop also addressed other issues of our process because it seemed more complicated to look at the issues of domestic violence with people from communities that are carrying such a profound historical grief around genocide.

And finally, one participant also had a low level of English language literacy. While she was able to develop a story, it was difficult for her in reading and recording the story. So that suggests more ethical considerations about how we would work in environments with adults who have limited literacy since so much of the work is formed around writing.

JL: There are a number of ethical considerations when you are working in resource-poor environments, and I think we have to be quite thoughtful about how the collaborators and the digital storytelling teachers communicate with participants about expectations, follow-up and the use of the stories. It is not a small irony to bring 21st century tools into environments that have 19th century infrastructures.

AH: Toward the future, we want to find a way to use the work in a broader context of community organizing, and to develop more consistent follow-up with the agencies we have worked with so we can figure out how to use the work on an ongoing basis.

Part of this is driven by the current media environment that continues to be filled with gratuitous images of women in positions of victimization and being terrorized. Not only that, but the approach of the so-called "women's" television that ends up portraying women as constantly being victims of stalking or domestic violence in this weird and creepy way. We feel compelled to put out a different version, people's *real* experiences, and create media that is driven by women and women of color that are so often under-represented or mis-represented in mainstream media.

And being able to inspire transformative personal experience, and provide access to tools in a way that simply would not work in other media access centers is what is powerful. The stories that have been created simply would not have been shared in a general digital video class.

JL: In thinking about this discussion for the book, it seemed that the lessons of this work would be relevant to discussions about doing work in the context of disability, life threatening disease, hospice care, etc. What are your thoughts on how this relates?

AH: Silence Speaks frames its work about the issues of violence and abuse, but people have responded to this in a number of ways. I think it is inappropriate to provide a stipulation to people that you must tell a story that is about an overt form of violence. As such, people have told stories from a number of angles that are more generally about healing. One woman made a piece that was tribute to her brother-in-law who died of AIDS. People have done stories about pregnancy and motherhood, sexuality and body image, which has a clear relationship to a history of violence and abuse and yet they are expressing this whole other constellation of issues.

Going back to the original impulse of this work, it is also about a strong belief in the power of art in the process of social change. When I go back and look at what inspired me and motivated me to take action and get involved, it has usually been art. A key part of our work is creating beauty out of situations that are not at all beautiful. In that way, in touching people at a core emotional level that will lead them to think in a new way and perhaps get involved and take action.

JL: There is a core theory in this work related to the larger cultural democracy, arts, and social change movements, in which there is an understanding that when people experience trauma, violence, and oppression, part of the process is a designification of their lives. The loss of power in being brutalized reflects itself in people feeling invisible. There is a feeling that there is no "sign" of their existence, which others in their families, their communities, their social world, need to heed. Cultural work is about re-signifying people, giving them tools to declare the value of their existence.

For better or worse, in our culture, there is a hierarchy of signifying presentation. At the top of that hierarchy is the screen; television and film. What I have seen is the actual lifting of spirit that occurs as people see their images, hear their voices, and connect their story to the medium of film. It is a particular dynamic or power that I don't believe is achieved in dance, music, theater, writing or visual arts presentations. It is regrettable that these historic forms have been diminished in their significance as communications media in our culture. But, as my friend Guillermo Gomez Peña has jokingly suggested, the new existential question is "TV or Not TV."

There have always been people that recognized this, filmmakers and video artists, who have gone up the training and technical ladder, and found the large financial resources to express themselves in this media, but the idea that filmmaking can be a general literacy, available to the mass of people, which is possible with the advent of this toolset, is profoundly different.

AH: Which is why a lot of filmmakers don't really know what to make of this work, and in my experience, are threatened by it, because it really breaks down the distinction between the people who are the creative professionals and the rest of us.

JL: Again we are talking about a relationship between the lay practitioner and a priesthood? The priesthood is very aware that its power is predicated on the obfuscation of the knowledge that they have. And obviously, we do not think this knowledge is mystical.

AH: Popular education practice is relevant here. In developing their own story and listening to others, people can make the links between their own struggle and the larger social struggle. Individual stories add up to the larger story. By starting with your own story and analyzing your own problems, a larger social consciousness is possible.

JL: But in doing digital storytelling we are saddled with the inelegant, feature–ridden toolset that is regrettably laden with the dominant cultural male attitude of the more toys, the more bells and whistles, the more value is invested in the tool.

AH: Which is why this work is so important with women and women of color because clearly a technophobia exists because of the perception that this is a male domain, and the fact that technology has been used against us in the past.

JL: Final thoughts?

AH: I feel that the work we are doing in helping to provide a transformative experience for survivors of violence links us to one end of the spectrum of the movements for social change. Being victimized by violence is a human rights violation. Allowing survivors to speak and have their stories heard heals all of us. And as we are healed, we can perhaps heal the world from its own cycles of violence.

14 Humanizing Healthcare

A Conversation with Pip Hardy and Tony Sumner, Pilgrim Projects/Patient Voices

A long our journey into digital storytelling, we have never been far from issues of health and well-being. Since our earliest workshops, stories of people's confrontation with severe illness, the journey through the health-care system, and recovery, have emerged. And given the call to meaning within our work, many stories have dealt with the loss of someone to illness, and have included narratives about the experience within different healthcare settings.

In the late nineties, we began to see initiatives in the healthcare field—organizations interested in stories of cancer survivors, the celebration of successful healthcare practices, disability, hospice care, and public health issues. In 2006, we learned of the Patient Voices program of Pilgrim Projects, a Cambridge, England-based organization that had begun to develop extensive healthcare work in digital storytelling. The deeply committed work of Pip Hardy and Tony Sumner has become an inspiration to all of us in the field.

Joe Lambert: How did you get involved in digital storytelling?

Pip & Tony: We have always used stories as an important element of the text-based and online education programs and learning materials we've developed over the last twenty-five years. In 2003, we were trying to bring the patient's voice into e-learning materials about healthcare quality improvement, and we stumbled across a community history digital story. It seemed to us that this digital technique of telling and sharing stories was the perfect way to convey the important stories of healthcare in a digital medium.

Our hope was that by bringing the very human element of stories back into healthcare education and service improvement programs, we could contribute to the huge task of humanizing a healthcare system that was increasingly characterized by targets and checkboxes, audits and statistics. We often have said that statistics tell us the system's experience of the individual, whereas stories tell us the individual's experience of the system.

JL: How did your work in Digital Storytelling evolve?

P & T: The main emphasis of our work has always been on the facilitation of others to tell their stories and share them digitally. We began working with individual patients and care-providers in late 2003, adopting a home-grown approach, and using very open questions to elicit a story about healthcare in relation to values such as equity, dignity, respect, trust, etc. At that point, it would be a further two years before we learned about CDS.

JL: So can you tell me something about making your own first digital stories?

P & T: Actually, our very first story was a collaborative effort between the two of us, facilitated by our friend Brendan Routledge in late 2003. It was a little piece, created in order to investigate the technology. It was a community history piece, but the community in question was the flock of doves in our back garden. It was driven by the images, which Pip assembled into a visual story using Windows MovieMaker. When the time came for recording, Tony ad libbed the voiceover and that was 'Dove Story'.

Eventually Pip discovered the existence of CDS as part of her research for her master's program and came to California to attend an introductory workshop in March 2006. It happened to be a facilitator-training workshop (although I was attending as a first-timer). My story was about my relationship with my father, who had died the previous year. Tony had found a picture of the house where I was born in an old Sunset magazine and that provided the prompt for the story. I remember being incredibly impressed with your comments when I sat with you, Joe. You seemed to understand exactly what I was trying to say.

As someone with a degree in English who has earned a living by writing for many years, developing the script wasn't too difficult for me, although the input from you, Emily, and others in the story circle was invaluable. But I did need a lot of help with Premiere and Photoshop—the use of layers still eludes me today—but was, of course, really pleased with the way the story came out. I learned a lot about my father—and myself—through making the story, and the real power of the digital storytelling workshop became apparent to me.

When I showed my story to my half-sister, Lucia, she decided she had to make one as well. She attended a workshop in June and then we both attended the next workshop designed especially for facilitators. My second story turned out to be a much darker piece than I had anticipated. I remember having heart palpitations for a couple of weeks before the workshop and I could barely breathe on the story circle day, but miraculously, since completing that story, there have been no more palpitations and I feel that creating that story helped me to walk past a particular dragon that prevailed over much of my life.

Tony's first story emerged from a masterclass held here in Cambridge with you and Emily in April of 2007. One of the reasons Pip and I work in concert together so well is the complementary and mutually supportive nature of our respective skills. As someone who has been involved in software industries since 1981, the technology is not a problem for me, but instead, an entertaining and intellectual puzzle or challenge.

As a sometime-physics graduate, creative writing has never figured obviously in my career path, although I have spent many years developing learning materials with Pip. So, for me the challenge and the benefit lies in the creation and perfection of the story script. Despite that, several of my stories have come, like the first one did, as one of those Eureka! moments at four in the morning.

Having worked on a story during the first day of the 'scar' prompt in the workshop, I found the space to reflect on scars and healing, and what they meant in my recent experience. When this reflection was combined with the catalytic and sharing input of other storytellers—some of whom were friends and colleagues—seeded and brought to life within me a story about how I had felt regarding my mother's very recent treatment for breast cancer.

I woke up early on the second morning scrabbling for a pencil and paper, wanting to write a story in which the language mirrored my experience of the inhuman, unfamiliar, specialized Latinate argot—mastectomy, unilateral, biopsy, etc.—that characterized for me the way that the medical establishment had used language to protect and distance itself whilst interacting with my mother.

I deliberately wrote the story using as few words as possible, to be delivered in a staccato and mechanical fashion because that was how I felt my mother's care had been, despite being clinically effective and, indeed, successful.

Although the story was still very present in my mind when I read it in the story circle on that second day, it was still a deeply reflective and affecting experience.

I've written several other stories since, but for me, the most enjoyable part of digital storytelling is actually in facilitating others in coming to terms (as I did) with their own experiences and emotions.

JL: In your own experience, why do you think digital storytelling is useful as a reflective practice?

P & T: For us there are three sides to the reflective prism that digital storytelling provides. First, there is the opportunity afforded to the viewer of a digital story to reflect on his or her own practice (and the practice of others). Sometimes seeing someone else's story about how they made a decision they might now regret can open the viewer's eyes to assess their own practice. This can be especially helpful for nurses, doctors and other people involved in healthcare. Second, there is the opportunity for storytellers to reflect on life experiences and consider the most effective and affective way of conveying their stories. Storytellers tell us that the process changes them. One initially quiet, even reticent, storyteller says, 'I feel as though I could talk to anyone now.' And we now have people coming back to make stories that are reflections of the impact that going through the digital storytelling process has had on their lives. And third, there is the opportunity for us as digital storytelling facilitators to reflect on our practice of DS facilitation and our own life experiences.

Also, our own reflective process has two main strands: The first strand is that our post-workshop wash-up meetings always reveal some small way in which we can better meet the needs of storytellers, whether through some smoothing of the technological first steps that they face, or through some refinements of the range of interpersonal skills and approaches that we use to engage storytellers and help them find the heart of their stories. The second strand of our program includes six weeks of once-weekly supervised meetings with an experienced counseling supervisor. It is in these reflective meetings that we are often able to identify issues of transference, and recognize where our own issues and experiences may be affecting our ability to be clear and available for storytellers. We feel these meetings are essential in maintaining our own psychological and emotional well-being, and the safety of the storytellers with whom we work.

As to why DS is so useful, we think it's a combination of things. Firstly, it's a bit like having three days—or twenty-four hours—of individual and group therapy! If we do our job right, people have the experience of being listened to and having their stories heard, often for the first time.

Digital storytelling and the rigorous process of script revision offers a wonderful opportunity to reflect on our own experiences, and those of others. Delving deeply into the meaning of a story, refining it, and distilling it to reveal its essence can help us to see it differently. Thich Nhat Hanh expresses it nicely:'*According to the law of reflection, the perceiver and the perceived have a very close link. When the angle of incidence changes, the angle of reflection will change immediately.*'

This process of distillation is a gradual process, with the story getting a bit stronger and then a bit stronger again until there is what one of our colleagues describes as a story characterized by 'purity, clarity and potency'—the characteristics of any good distillation! There is something about getting rid of much of the substance in order to get to the essence and people can then see the experiences of their lives with a new clarity.

Or put another way, stories spring from, and are linked to, people's past and current life experiences. Inevitably then, within the process of reflecting upon and distilling their digital story, storytellers are given the opportunity, space, and tools with, and within which, to reflect upon their own life stories. If they get to the essence of their story they usually have a better grasp of the essence of the experience.

There is also something about seeing the final story on the big screen at the end of the workshop—things hitherto buried are now out in the open and outside of the storyteller, creating a new kind of freedom. As one storyteller has said, *'When you've made your digital story, you don't have to hold it in your head any more. You can put it behind you and it doesn't take up any more space, so you can move on. You've named the beast."*

JL: What is unique to your approach to digital storytelling?

P & T: We have tried to take our original open and facilitative approach to education and blend it with the very best elements of CDS' approach, and with our particular mix of personal and professional skills and life experiences from counseling and groupwork, teaching, writing and editing, software development, educational materials design and project management to develop our own subtle variant of the process. We feel this is well suited to the vulnerable people with whom we work in health and social care—patients, service users, care-providers (and even clinicians and educators!).

As our original intention was always to create an educational resource, we have come at DS slightly differently, but because we also know that healing and learning are closely connected, we are able to combine the various elements that will, hopefully, contribute to both.

People have described our approach as caring, nourishing, and mindful, and we try very hard to ensure that those qualities are always present in every encounter.

JL: Pip can you tell us more about your background and how it has shaped your work?

P: Well, my background has been more in education than in therapy, although, as I said earlier, I think the two are closely linked. I've always been interested in non-traditional forms of education, those approaches that really help people to learn, rather than just pouring in information. So I trained as a Montessori teacher and eventually ended up in adult education, working firstly with unemployed and homeless people and then moving on to teach communication and what was once known in the UK as 'liberal studies'—an opportunity for people training to be hairdressers and bricklayers and carpenters to engage with movies and books and discussions about what makes us human. Gradually I moved into writing and editing open learning materials with a real focus always on the learner, and trying to find ways of translating the qualities of a good teacher—someone who motivates and stimulates and informs and encourages and guides and inspires and so on—into written words that would offer people who had missed out on education an opportunity to follow some of their dreams. Of course, I read Carl Rogers, and being a child of the sixties, I was pretty interested in self-development and becoming more aware. I became interested in Buddhism in the late seventies and that has really underpinned my life and work in different ways.

After working for quite a few years in education, I trained as a psychodynamic counselor and did some group work. I started training as a homeopath but practicalities meant that I had to return to the world of educational development. But the common themes running through all this have always been around looking at people as a whole—whether you are offering education or healing.

In fact, the dissertation I wrote for the counseling course was an exploration of different ways of viewing and understanding the self—from a Buddhist perspective and a psychodynamic perspective—and an attempt to see whether the two could work in harmony to promote healing. That was some time ago now, and Buddhist approaches are now commonly adopted in the talking therapies—but it wasn't so common back in the dim and distant past of the last century!

Buddhist practice, with its emphasis on being in the present moment and the need to be aware of what's going on in both body and mind, provides the foundation for cultivating understanding and compassion that are all too often missing in both education and healthcare. Such an approach affords an opportunity to link past experiences with current understandings, learning, and healing, and is essential to the functioning of a successful story circle—the core of our practice as DS facilitators. In all of these said traditions, stories play a huge part in leading people to new ways of understanding.

So, as our practice has developed, we have become aware from feedback and responses (and indeed, follow-up stories!), that many people experience the process in ways they describe as 'cathartic,' 'therapeutic,' 'retreat-like,' 'transformative,' and even 'spiritual." Whether this is partly due to the aspects of counseling, groupwork, and Buddhist practice that Pip brings to our work, or whether it's inherent in the DS process is debatable. I think that having an awareness of what may be going on for people is an important part of the role of any DS facilitator. If nothing else, it seems to make people feel safe to know that there is this strong ethical and therapeutic underpinning to our work. And, of course, if they feel safe, they are more likely to tell truly authentic stories.

JL: In healthcare, there are many concerns about patient's rights; protecting people's anonymity; not exploiting the suffering of others as part of the promotional efforts of healthcare agencies. How have you addressed these concerns?

P & T: Because of the area in which we work, and the nature of our storytellers, one of our key concerns has always been to wrap an appropriate and open ethical consent and release process around the digital storytelling experience which would protect and empower the storytellers, ensuring that they are able to give fully-informed consent at every stage of the process. So we have a three-stage consent and release process, which gives people plenty of time to think about whether they want to take part in a workshop, whether to release their story and whether to participate in the Patient Voices program.

In our experience, storytellers have almost always been very enthusiastic about their stories being given a wider audience. Objections to this have usually come from educational institutions and the medical establishment. People from these areas have often been concerned that what we were doing was 'research' and the stories should therefore be made anonymous. But the desire to be heard is very strong, and in the end, 'our hearts rebel against the heartlessness' of the researchers and the statisticians who would anonymize the stories of those who wish to tell them. Repeatedly, people choose voice over silence, and the heartfulness of a personal story over the heartlessness of a randomized control trial.

JL: As you mentioned, our healthcare systems—while seeking to heal and support others—often leave people feeling dehumanized and disempowered. Can you expand upon the issues of how storytelling helps to humanize healthcare?

P & T: Dehumanization takes many shapes, including restriction of access to health and social care services, poor quality care, inhumane care as well as terrible violence done to the human spirit by crushing a voice that wishes to be heard. We are fond of quoting James Earl Jones who says '*One of the hardest things in life is having words in your heart that you can't utter.*'

The majority of our storytellers are patients, professionals, or those involved in family care, and as such, a great many of them have stories of experiences that have been damaging to them or their loved ones. What they all have in common is a desire that, through the telling and sharing and dissemination of their stories, they can make a contribution towards the cessation of those experiences.

Storytellers certainly tell us that they are happy if, by sharing their story, someone else may be spared a similar experience. In that sense, I think people do feel they are contributing to the struggle to create a more humane and compassionate society. The notion of Ubuntu sums up pretty well what we are trying to do and why we are trying to do it:

'When I dehumanise you, I inexorably dehumanise myself. The solitary human being is a contradiction in terms and therefore you seek to work for the common good because your humanity comes into its own in belonging.'
—Bishop Desmond Tutu

JL: Even in our public workshops, people are willing to take risks with emotional material, and ordinarily they are prepared for the emotional impact of this work, but sometimes they are not. How do you address people's potential for going into crisis as part of the workshop experience?

P & T: Our primary concern is to ensure a place of safety for storytellers. We always have at least two facilitators, one of whom is a trained counselor (and the other makes sure the technology is always working!). In the event of a crisis, one person can stay with the group while the other supports the person in crisis.

We try to make the whole process a caring one, and where possible, that process begins several weeks before the actual workshop with an introductory briefing day for potential storytellers. We take this opportunity to show some stories, describe the process, explain the Patient Voices program, and do a little bit of story work. It gives people a chance to meet us and other storytellers, and to ask questions and make a well-informed decision about whether to attend the workshop. It also gives us a chance to assess things like literacy levels, technical ability, and emotional and mental states. This means that people who don't feel comfortable with any aspect of the process we've outlined need go no further while we, as facilitators, can make suitable preparations to ensure that the workshop is as comfortable and safe as possible for the participants.

We prefer to keep the groups small—usually six to eight storytellers—as we think this helps to create a comfortable, safe space in which to share personal stories.

We ensure that our facilitators are kept emotionally and psychologically fit through having supervision as well as through their own spiritual practices, including meditation, walking, motorcycle maintenance and other Zen-like and mindfulness-based activities.

Aided by our consent and release procedures, we strive to set clear guidelines for the group. We aim to provide a comfortable, holding and nourishing environment (physically, emotionally and spiritually), and to make a safe place or *temenos* (the Greek's concept of a sacred place for telling stories) within which storytellers can explore a range of feelings.

One of the things we do customarily is have dinner with storytellers on the night before a workshop begins. This offers an opportunity for us to break bread and drink wine (literally!), and to get to know one another. After dinner, we go through the program for the workshop and invite people to ask questions and air concerns so that they can begin the next morning with clear hearts and heads. We have observed that a well-formed group is very supportive of its members and this initial process of sharing seems to be quite important in helping the group to bond.

We may also invite people to share dinner with us on the second night if they wish to do so. It's an opportunity to relax a bit and we often take this time to show people more cheerful stories than those they are likely to have heard and seen—stories of joy and celebration, including some that we have made ourselves—and that's a way of letting people know us a little better. They can be reassured that we have walked the same road they are now walking.

We hope that our attempts to create this environment of safety reduces the risk of people going into crisis and, if they do, we make sure that one facilitator is available solely for that person.

We also keep in touch with people after the workshop ends. We let them know that they are now a part of the growing Patient Voices community of storytellers and that we will be contacting them. We always send out an email to everyone after a workshop, and we let them know in advance that we are going to do that. Sometimes that's enough to help people to feel reassured and safe. We thank them for their time and their stories and let them know roughly when we will be doing the post-production—this also links people up with one another, which most groups want. Sometimes people reply and let us know that they have been a bit shaky or wobbly in the first days after a workshop, so then we keep an extra eye on them (usually via email). We contact them again when the tidied versions of their stories are ready for their final approval.

If someone has told a particularly hard or painful story, we usually give them a call after a week or so to make sure they are ok. Some storytellers are keen to stay in touch, and we fall into an email correspondence. Several have joined in to become enthusiastic supporters of our humanizing healthcare initiative.

If we feel that someone is particularly vulnerable, we make an extra effort to maintain reasonably regular contact. Often the people who want to keep in touch are those who have experienced a real sense of transformation. They often make good use of their stories in their own work, want to go on to make other stories, and are great at spreading the word!

JL: Do you have an intuitive assessment of how your experience of working in these therapeutic contexts might be relevant to other areas of the health professions?

P & T: Our work was not originally intended to be therapeutic, nor were we working with storytellers for whom that was the main objective. Our intention was always to embed the stories in educational—and quality—improvement programs, conferences, and e-learning, in order to further our aim of humanizing healthcare through highlighting the human side of experience of health, illness, healthcare and the lack of it.

However, it becomes clearer with every workshop and from every storyteller's feedback that the process is inherently therapeutic. We know that digital storytelling is a powerful process and that digital stories can be powerful tools for learning and change. Like most powerful tools, we believe that DS needs to be used with care and knowledge, and understanding, and as you remind us, Joe, with love.

We find that people are quite creative in devising new uses for the stories. We have also noticed the wide relevance of any one story to other areas of the health service. Jimmy's story [patientvoices.org.uk/nhstay.htm], for example, is used by one lecturer we know to highlight deficiencies in record-keeping, patient safety, health inequalities, unnecessary transfers, professional behavior, and corporate liability—she can engage students in five or six lectures through the use of that one story!

The process of creating and sharing a digital story is definitely being taken up in a number of different areas of the health professions in the UK at least. So, for example, we have had junior doctors telling stories about clinical placements as a means of reflecting on their experiences. Newly qualified mental health nurses have told stories intended to be used in training their preceptors and for preparing future students for the reality of life after graduation.

Stories are being used to inform the design of services and devices for people with rheumatoid arthritis, and to share knowledge within and between organizations. Our sense is that people are slowly beginning to recognize the links between learning and healing. As more and more educators and clinicians come to make their stories, understanding is growing about the importance of careful reflection on experience and of listening and attending to patients as one human being to another—and that is the really therapeutic element for any of us.

JL: In the UK, and much of the world, "Complementary" or alternative therapies have gained greater acceptance. How would you position your work in the context of "Complementary" medical work?

P & T: Good question. We have neither tried to position ourselves as an opposition nor as an alternative to anything, but rather have tried to help all stake–

holders in health and social care heal the system from within. We want to build bridges rather than tear them down by recognizing that, as Tony has said, '...the ability to tell, hear and share stories of experience and aspiration is a prerequisite for the development of a learning organisation of reflective individuals."

We want to promote thoughtful use of language and mindful sharing of experiences. We seek to help people tell their stories not in an angry or aggressive way, but rather, in a way that will attract and hold the attention of those who devise and deliver healthcare without antagonizing them, while still retaining the integrity of the story and the storyteller.

Within the context of this question therefore, if DS is therapeutic, then it must be considered as a complementary therapy and a key component to the holistic approach to the patient, rather than an alternative one.

It is our strong view that facilitators need to be well-trained and experienced not just in digital storytelling, but in a range of other skills and knowledge bases, and in life experience and self-awareness—otherwise the wonderful alchemy that is digital storytelling at its best is likely to be diminished to little more than a Powerpoint presentation—as we've seen happen—where a formulaic use of digital technology takes precedence over the 'analog' storytelling and the distillation that results in something that is clear, pure and potent.

JL: The issue of access to healthcare in the UK and much of the developed world is quite different than it is here in the United States or in the developing world. We have attempted to link the struggle for voice of recipients of healthcare within our system, to expanded healthcare access. Do you have any thoughts about how the UK system is still challenged by issues of access, and how your work could be instrumental in bringing about change?

P & T: There is a universal health service in the UK, free for all at the point of need. But inevitably, given the social and economic variations across the country, health inequality remains an important issue. Health inequality for us encompasses not only inequality in access to or quality of healthcare services, but also inequality of voice and influence in the shaping and improvement of those services.

One of our original intentions with the Patient Voices program, and one of the reasons for its name, was to give a voice to those people who have waited patiently to be heard: those 'ordinary' people who come from all walks of life. We have worked with people from across the resource spectrum as well as with those on the edges of society and in 'hard-to-reach' communities including ethnic minorities, refugees and economic migrants, people disabled as a result of stroke or other cataclysmic events, people with mental health disorders and those who have been impoverished by disease or economic deprivation as well as the family members and friends who care for them.

By offering a voice to people who are seldom heard, and by distributing their stories as widely as possible, we are able to ensure that the stories are as widely heard as possible. It's really a kind of guerrilla advocacy, whereby the voices of ordinary people can be heard at the highest levels in the National Health Service and beyond.

From our monitoring of the website, we know that the stories are being widely used with the NHS as well as in medical schools and schools of nursing in many UK universities, which means that storytellers have a voice in the education of the next generation of healthcare professionals.

We are really pleased that some of the stories have been used, and hence given a platform, by the Chief Medical Officer and Chief Nursing Officer, and as well as the health minister, Lord Darzi. We have also worked on several projects with the National Audit Office, a body charged with auditing value for money in public sector spending. Their reports, and hence any accompanying Patient Voices stories, go directly to the Parliamentary Accounts Committee.

This means that the stories, and hence the storytellers, have the potential to affect healthcare policy. It may be coincidence, but we have noticed a greater emphasis on words like dignity, respect, and even humanity in policy documents. Patient involvement is now a statutory duty of healthcare organizations in the UK and several recent projects have focused on the benefits of patient involvement.

From a slightly different perspective, in our workshops we try to model the kind of ethos we would like to see in the health service, i.e., where everyone has an equal voice, and people are treated with respect and dignity.

We really do try to do it together (to quote Michael Gerrand's story), as part of the move toward patient empowerment, our own personal commitment to facilitative and participatory learning, and facilitative and participatory healthcare. Storytellers often remark on the novelty of being treated as equals—as people with something worthwhile to say; people worthy of respect, and they tell us that this experience of having their voices heard and valued gives them greater confidence and, perhaps, a new voice with which they can engage more effectively with healthcare providers and the system.

JL: In thinking about this discussion for the book, it seemed that the lessons of this work would be relevant to discussions about doing work in the context of disability, life threatening disease, hospice care, etc. What are your thoughts on how this relates?

P & T: Well, yes. That was the starting prompt in the small story circle of our digital storytelling work. Many of our friends, family members, and colleagues have had really terrible experiences of illness, disease and care. Working within the health sector and trying to ensure that patients really were at 'the heart of healthcare' as the UK Department of Health said they should be, presented us with the challenge that resulted in the Patient Voices program. We've now worked on projects covering all the areas that you mention. Stories of health, life, death, and disease can offer us deep insights into not only the storyteller, but the storytellers' family and cultural traditions—if only we are prepared to listen.

Our experience and observations are that, given the opportunity to reflect on, craft and shape their stories, storytellers feel empowered and enthusiastic about telling and sharing their stories. When given the opportunity to see and reflect on the stories, policy makers, deliverers and providers of care are deeply affected by them. In addition, it is particularly important to offer medical, nursing, and other healthcare students the opportunity to see, and where possible, create, their own stories of healthcare so that they begin to develop greater empathy for one another. When a group of final year medical students made stories, they commented on the powerfully reflective nature of the process and how it enabled them to see their patients more as human beings and less as opportunities for practicing new skills.

Our goal is to facilitate the telling and sharing of stories that are effective, affective and reflective (EAR) in that they are short, transmissible and distributable; compelling, honest and human; provocative, challenging, and mindful.

JL: Final thoughts?

P & T: A couple of things…It has come to our attention that many individuals and groups feel that they have the monopoly on suffering. People who have lost someone dear to them, people who are caring for a relative with a life threatening disease, people with psychosis, people who have been discriminated against, people who have been uprooted from their home; they think their situation is worse than someone else's.

But when you get a group of people together to share stories, there is a realization that we all suffer—it is just a part of the human condition; it is what we do with that suffering that is the really important thing.

And people realize that they can begin to transform their suffering by sharing it—first by articulating it to themselves, then to the small group, and perhaps, to the world. Then the sense of isolation and hopelessness begins to diminish, and a new hope is found in the community and communion of storytellers.

The next thing has to do with different kinds of knowledge. Here in the west we specialize in knowing stuff, learning things, analyzing, criticizing, and acquiring more knowledge. That's the knowledge of the intellect.

Gradually we are recognizing, with the help of people like Daniel Goleman, the Dalai Lama, and other Buddhist teachers, that it's important to balance intellectual knowledge with emotional knowledge. Indeed, as Ghandi said, 'the culture of the mind must be subservient to the culture of the heart.'

Going one step further, Parker Palmer, and doubtless many others, feel that there is a spiritual knowledge which informs the way we are in the world, and that is also crucial to our understanding of ourselves and others.

Finally, there is what we might call physical knowledge—knowledge of our bodies and how they work (or don't work) and why. There is much to be learned from our bodies.

Together, these four kinds of knowledge represent a holistic approach to knowing and might be called wisdom. We feel that the Patient Voices stories offer the opportunity to learn in these four different ways and have the capacity to contribute to a wiser, deeper, and more loving knowledge of humanity.

JL: And the third and final thing?

P&T: One of our most common observations and greatest joys over these years has been of the universality of stories and the commonality of shared experiences across, and within, workshop groups. We constantly see common themes—the themes of humanity—emerging.

"Each affects the other and the other affects the next, and the world is full of stories... and the stories are all one."
                                        —Mitch Albom, *The Five People You Meet in Heaven*

Thanks, Joe, for showing us the way.

Appendix A

The World of Digital Storytelling

While this book has emphasized the methods of training and production developed by the Center for Digital Storytelling, practitioners of Digital Storytelling could include anyone who has a high appreciation of the narrative arts (poetry, storytelling, theater, fiction, essays, film) who wants to create work on a computer. Below we discuss some of the possibilities and representative examples.

The Digital Storyteller in Performance

Theater and the performing arts have always integrated every available communication technology—from the use of recordings to state–of–the–art multimedia—while traditional storytellers have generally remained at the low–tech end of the innovation spectrum.

As such, Dana Atchley's *Next Exit* was a groundbreaking example of the integration of interactive media and the traditional performance storyteller. Over the last ten years, a number of other artists have developed plays and performances using the singular teller and digital media. Robert LePage's *Far Side of the Moon* was perhaps the most artistically ambitious solo show of the last decade, capturing the story of two brothers, cosmonaut Yagarin and the search for exterrestrial life, and meditations on human culture, into a fabulous mixture of moving set pieces and projection. Other artists who have worked successfully in a contemporary story form with technology include Rinde Eckert, Brenda Wong–Aoki, and Tim Etchells.

Beyond the context of traditional storytelling, many artists and organizations have explored digital applications in theater and performance. They have developed their work side-by-side with the engineers and technologists creating the newest tools of the Information Age. New York's Blue Man Group, Troika Ranch, and Laurie Anderson, San Francisco's George Coates Performance Works, England's

Builder's Association, Blast Theory, and Shinkansen, have addressed the impact of the Internet, cellular/wireless, distributed computing, and virtual reality in live performance. We have also seen a steady stream of work in new media and performance emerge from NYU, MIT Media Lab, Arizona State University, and the University of Texas at Austin.

Hypertext and Interactive Digital Storytelling

Since the early sixties, the goal of one segment of the information technology research community was to create a hypertextual environment to assist in the tasks of citation and referencing—an essential part of academic activity. At the same time, a number of academics interested in the potential literary applications of hypertext began collaborating on creating content. Since the mid-1980s, a number of hypertext novels, essays, and short stories were created, exploring a broad range of content. The hypertext movement also developed a series of tools and aesthetic principles to inform their work.

Our community of digital storytellers owes much of its perspectives about interactive narrative to the pioneering work of the hypertext community. Eastgate Systems in Boston has remained the center of both publication and dialogue about the hypertext community.

During the late 1990s in another corner of new media research, commercial application was the use of fixed media storytelling in laserdisc and then CD-ROM technologies. These efforts ushered in the era of interactive storytelling using rich, multiple media. Media professionals sought a new type of interactive, graphic publishing and new methods of virtual filmmaking. Research into these forms led to countless conceptual experiments, and there were many pioneers. These included Branda Laurel working in virtual reality with Placehoder, Abbe Don's *We Make Memories*, an exploration of four generations of women in her family, Pedro Meyer's *I Photograph to Remember*, documenting his parents' final struggle with cancer, Greg Roach's *I Am a Singer*, by Australian multimedia designer Megan Heyward, *Mauve Desert*, by Adrienne Jenek, *Ceremony of Innocence* (an adaptation of Nick Bantock's *Griffin and Sabine* trilogy), by Alex Mayhew, *Quantum Gate* and *X-Files* CD-ROMs, and Jon Sanborn's *Psychic Detective* CD-ROM.

This period culminated as researcher/theorists like Georgia Tech's Janet Murray developed literary theory to assess these narratives and their aesthetics (*Hamlet on the Holodeck*). And since the publication of earlier editions of this book, Carroll Parrott Blue's *The Dawn at My Back* memoir and DVD emerged as an exquisite and award-winning example of multimedia storytelling. But just as these arguments were becoming coherent, many of the pioneering practitioners were turning away from developing titles. An economy for fixed media storytelling was eclipsed by the Internet, and by the explosive growth of the gaming industry.

While games undoubtedly have narrative attributes, we have only met a small number of game developers who view the narrative concerns of their work as more than trivial. The success of the role-playing, puzzle–solving game, *Myst* demonstrated that significant attention to story could make a huge difference in how an audience responds to the "puzzle" aspects of a game. Many adventure game developers consider themselves constructing "storied" worlds—plausible characters reacting in plausible ways to plausible circumstances (within the genre).

In all of these interactive narratives, like their hypertext equivalents, navigational design is a critical part of aesthetic success or failure. The more artistically successful have a consistent navigational mechanism for the users to stay in touch with the story arc. In games based on *Harry Potter* or *Lord of the Rings*, users see an adventure through to its conclusion with the defeat of an evil enemy. These games also create a dialogue with the user that deepens or extends the user's emotional connection to the story line—narrative bridges that establish the next level of game play—either by calling for their direct participation as characters who can shape the story's resolution, or in inquiring about the user's response to material that is presented.

My son is a typical gamer: for him the narrative set up gets in the way of game play. He usually skips it. In general, game developers and interactive designers agree that what we mean by story, the author's intended "best" route for the audience through the narrative, is not the role of games (chess, basketball, *Halo 2*). In games, users follow their own route, making their own story in the process. Whether the story they end up experiencing is dramatically and emotionally compelling is not necessarily the player's priority. In this way, good storytelling and good interactivity or game play, are often in conflict.

Diaries, Blogging, Podcasting, and Social Media

The day after the Internet came to be, the online diary existed. People naturally used e-mail, bulletin boards, newsgroups, and of course, the greater capabilities of the Web to publish creative writing about their life experience. An online writer's notebook made immediately available to an audience had two fundamentally attractive characteristics that traditional writing lacked: instant feedback, and an inexaustible potential for connections and direct dialogue with an audience. Justin Hall traveled the country and world documenting his life for an internet audience on *Links.net* (1994–2004). His work became prototype for what has become a major hobby worldwide. Technorati.com currently tracks 33 million blogs, and the number is constantly growing. The majority take the form of diarist sites, recounting daily experience as stories and reflections. As these move to radio and video through podcasting, webcams, and online personal photo/video/audio databases, the form expands to an endless array of expressive possibilities. The development of these media tend to blur the cultural boundaries between insight and exhibitionism, intimacy and self-absorption, reasoned discourse and individualistic banter; but they are clearly becoming the most ascendent form of publication in the world.

Derek Powazek's *the fray* (1996–2005) approached this phenomena with more artful intentions: curating personal essays on many topics that directly invite readers to respond with personal stories of their own. This type of storytelling interaction encourages community, connecting diverse people through shared experience. We look forward to the continued growth of communities of writers exploring the internet as a mechanism of self–awareness and ever more effective storytelling.

In the time between the second and third editions of this textbook, the methods for connecting artists, diarists, and citizens with audiences have blossomed with the advent of social networking sites like MySpace and Facebook, and modified blogging tools like Tumblr and Twitter. As a digital storyteller, social media sites are excellent opportunities to spread the word about screenings and events, to send followers and friends to the web–based locations of your stories, and these sites are even conduits by which you can directly share your stories. The digital world moves at lightspeed, and by the time you are reading this there will certainly be new techno-fads and tools with which you can experiment.

Place–Based Mobile Storytelling

The future of digital storytelling is undoubtedly going to be mobile devices. The cell phone of the near future will have a hard drive and function as a multimedia computer with a simple attachment to tie it to a monitor, and wireless connections to mouse and keyboard. One of the advantages of the truly portable computer will be that it can help us to meet the ghosts that linger in all places.

Our colleagues in Canada developed Murmur in 2003, as a way to capture community stories. The idea was relatively simple, record interviews with people about buildings, stores, neighbors, parks, whatever comes up about a place, and then organize the interviews into a walking tour of the neighborhood. The stories could be heard on a cell phone, and signs were strategically placed around neighborhoods that simply read, "Murmur," and listed a phone number and a code. At the other end of the call was a big answering machine. You could call the number, and a voice would say, "Look over to the right, and in this house, forty years ago was a group of Zen Buddhist militants…." There are now many projects like this.

This portends a world where all places have stories imbedded in them. Not official stories, or perhaps those, but also contemporary stories, oral histories, memorials, and calls to remembrance. And you will not only listen, you will leave your own, and they will amalgamate in an enormous GoogleEarth database so that all places on the entire planet will have a residue of memory, available at the push of a button, with sound, and pictures, and digital stories in multiple automatically translated languages. This is not a wild idea, but totally feasible in the coming five years.

And what it means is that we will never again be a total stranger to a place. Because being a local means that these stories are part of you, the ghosts of the past are with you, and their memory lives in the park benches and porches. If you can call them up, to know that this is the house where John passed away, the man who once saved a cat from a fire. If you know that, then you know you are someplace special, wherever you are.

This could change the world.

Appendix B

Creating a Digital Storytelling Production Environment

When asked about the shopping list for establishing either a computer lab or personal workstation for producing digital stories, my answer is always the same: "How much money do you have?"

Digital video production is more affordable than ever. New and used PC and Mac machines capable of running digital video editing software are readily available. Digital media tools have greatly evolved, but much is left to be done to bring elegance and consistency to the marketplace. However, professional software is becoming increasingly stable and reliable with each version, though minors changes within each application do occur, such as where selector tools and menus are located on a user's screen. But despite these changes, the influx of consumer-level solutions presents a multitude of interface design metaphors to choose from.

We have tended to lean towards a small set of system and software solutions depending on the environments we are working in. As a non-profit arts organization with financial constraints, we like most of you, have made choices, based on necessity, trial and error, and market research.

We would like to now outline the issues and approaches that we take to the present digital media environment.

In our workshops, and with our partners, our labs consist of the following ingredients:

- One laptop or desktop computer per storyteller
- A facilitator's computer connected to a projector with speakers
- A digital camera for capturing still images
- A digital video camera
- One to two sets of audio recording equipment
- One flatbed scanner
- A networked printer available for printing storytellers' scripts
- Image, video, audio and other software
- Data storage

Let's review each of these components.

Workstations

In 2009, most computers can handle video recording and playback at consistent levels. If you're looking at buying used machines, they should have a minimum of 1 GB RAM and a 80 GB hard drive. However, 100 GB or greater of hard drive space helps to satisfy the voracious appetite for video, which runs at almost 210 MB per minute, or 13 GB per hour at highest resolution. Video remains one of the most demanding applications for a computer, so if it can handle the minimum requirement of your video editing software application, it can handle about any other software you are going to throw at it in the digital story production process.

Each workstation should have a pair of headphones, and even if the computers you are using are laptops, then we highly recommend outfitting each with a mouse as well. While the trackpad is convenient, a mouse helps with some of the more intricate editing that will take place in the later stages of the editing process.

Digital Cameras

If you have been using a 35mm film camera and scanning images, and then switch to a digital camera at a price point below $500, it would not surprise us if you went back to film. But digital cameras are improving daily, and they provide numerous arguments for their ease of use and economy in a multimedia environment. If you have the money now, or can wait another two years, the inexpensive digital camera really will be compatible in quality with film cameras of a similar price. As for brands, we have liked our Nikon Coolpix, but the Olympus, Canon, and Minolta cameras all seem comparable.

Digital Video Cameras

This is another competitive world in which consumers benefit from the nature of the current marketplace. DV has three levels of cost/quality in the current market: sub–$1000, $1000–$2000, and above $2000. The average sub–$1000, or consumer level camera, is extraordinary for the price, and will service almost any family, school, or home use. In the middle range, cameras offer more feature sets, more compactness, and slightly better quality. Above $2000, you begin to have near-professional quality, with such features as balanced audio, for example. Feature films are being shot with the Canon GL2, Sony FX–1, or the Panasonic DVX–100a or b cameras for around $3000 or less, so I can't think why anyone would spend more than this on a camera who is not fully in the film business.

Audio Capture

The ability to record onto a computer is now standard on most PCs and MACs, but Apple still makes it a bit easier than the PC. To capture audio on a PC, we suggest Adobe's Audition, Bias Peak, and Sony's Sound Forge. On a Mac, you can use Sound Studio Pro, GarageBand, and even the native Quicktime Pro.

For audio equipment, we recommend a Shure 58 with a windsock, a mic stand, small mixer (Mackie's least–expensivce model is sufficient), and appropriate cables. At this point, USB microphones (Audio Technica and Blue) are also an option, though they do not have the warmth of an analog microphone. We have found that the combination of a Shure 58 mic and a Mackie mixer offer optimal quality and reliability in the current market.

Scanning/Image Production

Adequate flatbed scanners can often be purchased for under $100, and are often given away for free when you purchase a new computer, but if you're looking to buy a new scanner, we recommend Canon scanners because of their reliability. Most scanners come with their own built-in software, but we recommend either full Photoshop or Photoshop Elements for scanning and editing images. In a pinch, a digital camera in good lighting can be used in place of a scanner to digitize images.

Video Software

On the Mac side of things, Final Cut Express is an ideal choice if budgets allow. Final Cut Pro, if there are no budgetary retraints. On the PC side, Sony Vegas Movie Studio and Adobe Premier Elements offer similar toolsets to Final Cut Express, though cost slightly less. If a larger budget is available, Sony Vegas Pro and Adobe Premier Pro offer an equivalent to Final Cut Pro for slightly less as well.

In addition to these industry standards, there are a number of other consumer-level toolsets being developed for Mac and PC, as well as online and open–source applications for constructing simple, narrated slideshows with few bells and whistles.

Other Software

We live and die by two post-production softwares, Autodesk Cleaner and Roxio's Toast Titanium. The first, Cleaner, is what compresses batches of movies to prepare them for CD-ROM, DVD, Web, or other uses. The second, Roxio, helps to burn the hundreds of CDs and DVDs we use to store material. DVD authoring, podcasting and integrated media and web design packages, like the extraordinary iLife softwares by Apple, are now considered de riguer for the Digital Storyteller. You can now make DVDs or web publish your movie quickly and easily. Of course word processing and Web applications should be available in the lab, for scripting and research.

Data Storage and Archiving

It is not a good idea to do video production on a server across a network, so having a local data storage system for production is critical. We use flash drives for transferring files during workshops, and portable, external firewire hard drives to back-up data during and after workshops. Furthermore, during and after post production for data archive and redundancy, we recommend using much larger (2 TB) hard drives and a server.

Spending Money

Another lesson we've learned is to never buy the latest, coolest product when it's first released, whether software or hardware. This is because the designers always get it wrong at first, and then fix it for about six months. Your machine has a reasonable shelf life of two–to–five years. And in an effort to reduce waste and save on your spending, perfectly reliable used machines can be purchased with warranties from reputable vendors.

It's important to remember that if you're planning to set yourself up with a complete digital storytelling lab, and have a limited budget, you can approach the above list of items in phases. However, if you are looking to purchase everything at once, expect to spend in the neighborhood of $25,000 to $35,000 for a lab of ten to twelve storytelling workstations.

The Computing Appliance: A Final Editorial Note

In chapter two, the argument was made that we are moving towards a memory box that helps us store our memories and reflect on our experiences. In 2009, the memory box has become the Smart Mobile Phone. Blackberrys and iPhones can take pictures, record audio, shoot video, and upload files to websites. That being said, the computer and mobile phone industries still do not think of elegance as a design feature. Bells and whistles and apps galore are what sells the devices, and as such the never ending problem of version creep (built in obsolesence of hardware, software and operating systems), and vaporware, or software and hardware rushed onto the market before the products are fully functional, persists.

When you buy a device to make media you have the choice of waiting until the bugs are shaken off, meaning six months after the release, or holding out for some enormous breakthrough in the technology that lowers the price and increases the quality. The truth is, you can't "win" with technology, but with a healthy dose of creativity, you can make great art with what you have. So whether you buy the cool new toy, or borrow a neighbor's old computer, make the best of it. If it drives you crazy, don't take it too personally, you are far from alone.

Appendix C

Web Resources for Digital Storytelling

Principal Resource Sites

1. Center for Digital Storytelling
www.storycenter.org
The online home of CDS. On our site you can access sample stories created in our workshops, case studies of projects we have partnered with other organizations, links to our other published resources, and information about our offices and workshops around the United States, Canada, and the world. Through our site you can also access the following, additional resources:

Story Circles
www.storycircles.org
A user-generated collection of digital stories covering a broad range of topics. You can join the Story Circle community to upload your own stories and watch and comment on stories that other users have posted.

StoryMapping Stories
www.storymapping.org
A project marrying digital storytelling with digital mapping to create story-based GoogleMaps, cell phone walking tours, Windows Live virtual tours, and stories embedded into specific locations that can be viewed using Bluetooth and other wireless technologies.

2. Stories for Change
www.storiesforchange.net
An online meeting place for digital storytelling facilitators and advocates to share stories and curriculum ideas, and to start dialogs about storytelling.

3. Educational Uses of Digital Storytelling
www.digitalstorytelling.coe.uh.edu
An amalgamation of resources on the educational uses of digital storytelling.

4. Hillary McLellan's Story Link
www.tech-head.com/dstory.htm
Researcher, educator, and digital storyteller, Hillary McLellan's, site has the most comprehensive database of digital story links on the Web.

Broadcast and Large Scale Institutions

1. Capture Wales
Cardiff, Wales
www.bbc.co.uk/wales/capturewales
Trained by the Center for Digital Storytelling, BBC in Wales/Cymru developed an ongoing program in digital storytelling that has continued to collect hundreds of stories from throughout the country of Wales.

2. Australian Center for the Moving Image
Melbourne, Australia
www.acmi.net.au
A public story showcase with a range of projects working with immigrant and indigenous communities, families facing Alzheimer's disease, and other chronic health issues.

3. Delta Garden
Vaxjo, Sweden
www.deltagarden.se
A regional project to collect digital stories throughout Sweden and to develop other methods for the promotion of citizen media production.

4. Digital Clubhouse Network
Sunnyvale, California, USA
www.digiclub.org
A program capturing stories of youth, elders, women, people with disabilities, and non-profit health and social service organizations.

5. Museum of the Person
Sao Paulo, Brazil
www.museudapessoa.net/ingles
An oral history program that collects, archives, and exhibits every-day life stories by Brazilians.

CDS Case Studies in Health and Human Services

1. Amplifying Voices
Johannesburg, South Africa
www.soros.org/resources/multimedia/digital
A workshop in Johannesburg for women and men from the Southern African Development Community countries who are especially vulnerable to HIV and AIDS.

2. Critical Condition
Denver, Colorado, USA
www.rmpbs.org/panorama/index.cfm/entry/342/Health-Care-Video-Stories
A program to help enable viewers of Critical Condition, a documentary examining the "broken" US healthcare system, to create digital stories about their own healthcare experiences.

3. HopeLab: Stories by Young Cancer Survivors
San Francisco, CA, USA
www.hopelab.org/innovative-solutions/digital-storytelling
In collaboration with CDS, HopeLab brought young cancer survivors from across the U.S. to participate in a digital storytelling workshop in order to better understand the needs and interests of young people who have survived cancer.

4. "Learn From My Story": Women Confront Fistula in Rural Uganda,
Masaka, Uganda
www.engenderhealth.org/our-work/maternal/digital-stories-uganda-fistula.php
A digital storytelling project for Ugandan women who have experiences obstetric fistula.

5. Men as Partners
Johannesburg and Cape Town, South Africa
www.engenderhealth.org/our-work/gender/digital-stories-south-africa.php
A promotional project to help involve men in gender equality and HIV/AIDS prevention and care work.

6. Nurstory: Digital Stories from the Colorado University School of Nursing
Denver, Colorado, USA
www.milehighstories.com/?page_id=21
Interdisciplinary stories from doctors, nurses, and patients at the Colorado University School of Nursing.

7. Preparation for Adulthood, Supervising for Success
New York, New York, USA
www.hunter.cuny.edu/socwork/nrcfcpp/pass/digital-stories/index.htm
The Hunter College School of Social Work's project to bring together current and former foster youth and social workers to share their experiences through digital storytelling.

8. Y.O.U.T.H. Training Project
California; Hawaii, USA
www.youthtrainingproject.org
A project bringing current–and–former foster youth together to share stories of their lives in order to build leadership, and improve child welfare practice.

CDS Case Studies in Environmental and Social Justice

1. "A Better Life Than Me": Stories of Labor Migration in Southern Africa
Johannesburg, South Africa
www.youtube.com/iompretoria
Digital stories that recount the hardships and celebrations of Sub-Saharan laborers.

2. Cows & Fish: Stories from Canada's Alberta Riparian Habitat Management Society
Alberta Province, Canada
www.cowsandfish.org/photos/digital.html
A digital storytelling project, that documents landowner's stories about their experiences in land management and their relationship with the land.

3. Progressive Communicators Project
Portland, Oregon, USA
www.pcn-nw.blip.tv/#1423118
A digital storytelling workshop for organizers and advocates from grassroots social and economic justice initiatives in Oregon, Washington, and Idaho.

4. Silence Speaks
Australia, Brazil, Canada, South Africa, Uganda, USA
www.silencespeaks.org
Digital storytelling in support of healing and violence prevention.

5. Somali Bantu Refugees Speak
Washington, DC, USA
www.afsc.org/somalibantu
Digital stories describing the challenges of forced migration, refugee camp life, and eventual resettlement in the U.S.

6. The Story Project of Central Neighborhood House
Toronto, Ontario Province, Canada
www.thestoryproject.ca
A digital storytelling project inviting immigrant women to reclaim media technologies, while also catalyzing community development and organization.

7. Sonke Gender Justice Network
South Africa
www.genderjustice.org.za/projects/digital-stories.html
Digital storytelling workshops that seek to achieve gender equality, reduce gender-based violence, and reduce the spread of HIV and AIDS.

CDS Case Studies in Arts, Culture, and History

1. The Container Project
Plamer's Cross, Clarenden, Jamaica
www.container-project.net
A digital storytelling workshop reaching across rural parts of Jamaica, and acting as a starting point for the establishment of a new media movement throughout the island.

2. My Place Project
San Francisco and San Rafael, California, USA
www.cafilm.org/education/myplace.html
In this project, location-based photography and video are used to assist in place-based digital stories made by San Francisco and Marin County youth.

3. Painted Bride
Philadelphia, Pennsylvania, USA
www.paintedbride.org/experience-more/digital-storytelling
This project supports youth in their stories about violence and other struggles within their communities.

Placed-Based Storytelling Resources

1. Murmur
www.murmurtoronto.ca
Canadian project which grew to international movement of cell phone based community story sharing.

2. Wayfaring
www.wayfaring.com
A tool for creating walking tours in google maps.

3. The Organic City
www.theorganiccity.com/wordpress
Oakland prototype of community story tours.

4. Guide By Cell
www.guidebycell.com/gbc/tour.jsp#walkingtours
Guide by Cell creates systems for audio guides using cell phones.

5. PlaceStories
www.placestories.com
PlaceStories is a software system for managing digital media, creating digital stories and publishing online.

6. Geo Graffiti
www.geograffiti.com
A tool to allow mobile phone users to openly express, share, aggregate, and retrieve local opinions in voice form.

7. Forgotten Ithaca
www.forgottenithaca.wordpress.com
A great example of a place-based blog.

CDS Case Studies in K–12 and Higher Education

1. The Digital Hero Book Project
Cape Town, South Africa
www.digitalherobook.org
A youth-based, international and inter-classroom exchange of digital stories aimed at developing literacy, and digital media skills.

2. Downtown Aurora Visual Arts
Denver, Colorado, USA
ww.davarts.org/art_storiesB.html
A summer youth program for middle school students to take part in digital storytelling.

3. Guardian Scholars
Berkeley, California, USA
www.calstate.fullerton.edu/news/2005/storytelling.html
A collection of digital stories created by former foster youth who received full tuition and expenses as part of the Guardian Scholar program at California State University Fullerton.

4. "The Project": Another School and Another Community Are Possible
Watsonville, California, USA
www.communitytv.org/programs/online/whats-happening-education-pt-1-0
A digital storytelling initiative intended to prompt dialogue among students, parents, teachers, and university faculty about how poverty and oppression impede upon a variety of different sociopolitical issues.

5. Streetside Stories' Tech Tales
San Francisco, California, USA
www.streetside.org/stories/digital-stories.htm
A partnership between CDS and Streetside Stories that yielded a digital storytelling project involving 300 7th graders.

6. T–TEC: Trans-Bay Training and Education Collaborative
San Francisco and Alameda Counties, California, USA
www.ccsf.edu/Resources/TTEC/about.html
A program using digital stories as an outreach tool to recruit new students into social service training programs.

7. University of Maryland, Baltimore County
www.umbc.edu/digitalstories
A digital storytelling training program for University of Maryland's faculty and staff.

8. Digital Storytelling at Ohio State University
www.telr.osu.edu/storytelling

9. Digital Storytelling at the University of Wisconsin
www.digitalstorytelling.doit.wisc.edu

10. Digital Storytelling at Williams College
www.digitalstorytelling.doit.wisc.edu

11. Digital Storytelling at the University of Oslo
www.intermedia.uio.no/mediatized

International Programs

1. Patient Voices
www.patientvoices.org.uk
UK-based Digital Storytelling project in Healthcare.

2. Untold Stories
www.untoldstories.eu
European library network working with immigrant voices.

3. Digi-tales
www.digi-tales.org
European wide Digital Storytelling project.

Design Examples

1. Dana Atchley's Next Exit
www.nextexit.com
Home of Dana's archive and background on his work in professional and artistic contexts.

2. Creative Narrations
Seattle, Washington, USA
www.creativenarrations.net
Community-based storytelling resource in Somerville, Massachusetts.

3. The Photobus
www.photobus.co.uk
The digital stories, photographs, and tutorials of photographer and storyteller Daniel Meadows.

4. Zone Zero
 www.zonezero.com
Pedro Meyer has created a quintessential photography site featuring fascinating work from around the world.

Technology Resources

TechSoup
www.techsoup.org
Non Profit resource for digital media projects large and small, access to low-cost software for non-profits.

50 Ways to Tell a Web 2.0 Digital Story
www.cogdogroo.wikispaces.com/50+Ways
A wonderful guide to web–based digital storytelling.

Creative Commons
www.creativecommons.org
Links to the numerous public source media, images in flckr, music from Jamendo, video from *archive.org*, etc.

Casting Words
www.castingwords.com
An online transcription service.

Bibliography

Digital Storytelling

Hartley, John and Kelyy McWilliam. *Story Circle: Digital Storytelling Around the World*. New York: Wiley-Blackwell, 2009.

Howell, Dusti and Deanne Howell. *Digital Storytelling: Creating an eStory*. Santa Barbara, CA: Linworth, 2003.

Johnson, Steven. *Interface Culture*. San Francisco: HarperSanFrancisco, 1997

Laurel, Brenda. *Computers As Theatre*. Menlo Park, CA: Addison-Wesley, 1993

Lundby, Knut. *Digital Storytelling, Mediatized Stories: Self-representations in New Media*. New York: Peter Lang Publishing, 2008.

Murray, Janet H. *Hamlet on the Holodeck: The Future of Narrative in Cyberspace*. New York: The Free Press, 1997.

Ohler, Jason B. *Digital Storytelling in the Classroom: New Media Pathways to Literacy, Learning, and Creativity*. New York: Corwin Press, 2007.

Porter, Bernajean. *DigiTales: The Art of Digital Storytelling*. Ballston Spa, NY: BP Consulting, 2004.

Sloane, Sarah. *Digital Fictions: Storytelling in a Material World*. New York: Ablex Corp., 2000.

Snyder, Ilana. *Page to Screen: Taking Literacy into the Electronic Age*. London: Routledge, 1998.

Standley, Mark and Skip Via. *Digital Storytelling with iMovie/Powerpoint*. Visions Technology in Education, 2004.

Storytelling, Story Work, and Public Speaking

Birch, Carol L., and Melissa A. Heckler, eds. *Who Says? Essays on Pivotal Issues in Contemporary Storytelling: American Storytelling from August House*. Little Rock, AR: August House Publishers, 1996.

Cassady, Marsh. *The Art of Storytelling: Creative Ideas for Preparation and Performance*. Colorado Springs, CO: Meriwether Publishing, 1994.

Cox, Allison M. and David H. Albert. *The Healing Heart: Storytelling to Build Strong and Healthy Communities*. Gabriola, BC: New Society Publishers, 2003.

Davis, Donald. *Telling Your Own Stories.* Little Rock, AR: August House Publishers, 1993.

Mooney, Bill, and David Holt. *The Storyteller's Guide.* Little Rock, AR: August House Publishers, 1996.

Polletta, Francesca. *It Was Like a Fever: Storytelling in Protest and Politics.* Chicago: University of Chicago Press, 2006.

Robbins, Jo. *High Impact Presentations: A Multimedia Approach.* New York: John Wiley and Sons, 1997.

Tilly, Charles. *Stories, Identities, and Political Change.* Lanham, Md. : Rowman & Littlefield, 2002.

Creative Writing and Autobiography

Atkinson, Robert. *The Gift of Stories : Practical and Spiritual Applications of Autobiography, Life Stories, and Personal Mythmaking.* Westport, CT: Bergin & Garvey, 1995.

Case, Patricia Ann. *How to Write Your Autobiography: Preserving Your Family Heritage.* Santa Barbara, CA: Woodbridge Press, 1995.

Egri, Lajos. *The Art Of Dramatic Writing: Its Basis In The Creative Interpretation Of Human Motives.* Rockford, IL: BN Publishing, 2009.

Goldberg, Natalie. *Writing Down the Bones: Freeing the Writer Within.* Boston: Sambala, 1986.

Lamott, Anne. *Bird by Bird: Some Instructions on Writing and Life.* New York: Pantheon Books, 1994.

Maquire, Jack. *The Power of Personal Storytelling.* New York, Tarcher–Putnum, 1998.

Metzger, Deena. *Writing for Your Life: Discovering the Story of Your Life's Journey.* San Francisco: Harper Collins, 1992.

Polking, Kirk. *Writing Family Histories and Memoirs.* Cincinnati, OH: Betterway Books, 1995.

Rainer, Tristine. *Your Life As Story.* New York: G.P. Putnam's Sons, 1997.

Roorbach, Bill. *Writing Life Stories: How To Make Memories Into Memoirs, Ideas Into Essays And Life Into Literature.* 2nd Edition. New York: Writers Digest Books, 2008.

Selling, Bernard. *Writing From Within: A Guide to Creativity and Life Story Writing.* Alameda, CA: Hunter House, 1988.

Stone, Richard. *The Healing Art of Storytelling: A Sacred Journey of Personal Discovery.* New York: Hyperion, 1996.

Design and Applications

Bone, Jan, and Ron Johnson. *Understanding the Film: An Introduction to Film Appreciation.* 4th edition. Lincolnwood, IL: NTC, 1995.

DuChemin, David. *Within the Frame: The Journey of Photographic Vision.* Berkeley, CA: New Riders Press, 2009.

Horn, Robert. *Visual Language: Global Communication for the 21st Century.* Bainbridge Island, WA: Macrovu Inc., 1999.

McCloud, Scott. *Reinventing Comics: How Imagination and Technology Are Revolutionizing an Art Form.* New York: Perennial, 2000.

McCloud, Scott. *Understanding Comics: The Invisible Art.* New York: Kitchen Sink Press, 1993.

McDonagh, Deana, Paul Hekkert, Jeroen van Erp, Diane Gyi eds. *Design and Emotion.* Boca Raton, FL: CRC Press, 2003.

McKee, Robert. *Story; Substance, Structure, Style and the Principles of Screenwriting.* New York: It Books (Harper Collins), 1997.

Powazek, Derek. *Design for Community.* Berkeley, CA: New Riders Press, 2002.

Shedroff, Nathan. *Experience Design.* Berkeley, CA: New Riders Press, 2001.

Withrow, Steven. *Secrets of Digital Animation: A Master Class in Innovative Tools and Techniques.* Hove, England: RotoVision, 2009.

Storytelling and Education

Alterio, Maxine. *Learning Through Storytelling in Higher Education: Using Reflection and Experience to Improve Learning.* London: RoutledgeFalmer, 2003.

Bell, Lee Anne. *Storytelling for Social Justice: Connecting Narrative and the Arts in Antiracist Teaching.* London: Routledge, 2010.

Bruner, Jerome. *The Culture of Education.* Cambridge, MA: Harvard University Press, 1996.

Egan, Kieran. *Teaching As Story Telling: An Alternative Approach to Teaching and Curriculum in the Elementary School.* Chicago: The University of Chicago Press, 1986.

Egan, Kieran. *The Educated Mind: How Cognitive Tools Shape our Understanding.* Chicago: The University of Chicago Press, 1997.

Fields, Anne M. and Karen R. Diaz. *Fostering Community through Digital Storytelling: A Guide for Academic Libraries.* Santa Barbara, CA: Libraries Unlimited, 2008.

Frazel, Midge. *Digital Storytelling Guide for Educators*. International Society for Technology in Education, 2010.

Cognitive Theory, Psychology, and Narrative

Carson, Jo. *Spider Speculations: A Physics and Biophysics of Storytelling*. New York : Theatre Communications Group, 2008.

Dennett, Daniel C. *Kinds of Minds: Toward an Understanding of Consciousness*. New York: Basic Books, 1996.

Fireman, Gary D., Ted E. McVay, Owen J. Flanagan. *Narrative and Consciousness: Literature, Psychology and the Brain*. New York: Oxford University Press (USA), 2003.

Gardner, Howard. *Frames of Mind: The Theory Of Multiple Intelligences*. New York: Basic Books, 1993.

Goleman, Daniel. *Emotional Intelligence: Why It Can Matter More Than IQ*. New York: Bantam Books, 1995.

Gubrium, Jaber F. *Analyzing Narrative Reality*. Thousand Oaks, CA: SAGE, 2009.

Harvey, John H. *Embracing Their Memory: Loss and the Social Psychology of Storytelling*. Needham Heights, MA: Allyn and Bacon, 1996.

Hunt, Celia. *Therapeutic Dimensions of Autobiography in Creative Writing*. London: Jessica Kingsley Publishers, 2000.

Kast, Verena. *Folktales as Therapy*. New York: Fromm International, 1995.

Kurtz, Ernest. *The Spirituality of Imperfection: Storytelling and the Search for Meaning*. New York: Bantam, 1992.

Linde, Charlotte. *Life Stories: The Creation of Coherence*. Oxford: Oxford University Press, 1993.

McAdams, Dan P. *The Stories We Live By: Personal Myths and the Making of the Self*. New York: Guilford Press, 1993.

Ong, Walter J. *Orality and Literacy: The Technologizing of the Word*. London: Routledge, 1982.

Parry, Alan and Robert E. Doan. *Story Re-Visions: Narrative Therapy in the Post-Modern World*. New York: The Guilford Press, 1994.

Schank, Roger C. *Tell Me a Story: Narrative and Intelligence*. Evanston, IL: Northwestern University Press, 1990.

Storytelling in Corporate and Organizational Contexts

Boje, David Michael. Storytelling Organizations. Thousand Oaks, CA: SAGE Publications Ltd, 2008.

Brown, John Seely et al. *Storytelling in Organizations: Why Storytelling Is Transforming 21st Century Organizations and Management.* Boston: Butterworth–Heinemann, 2004.

Denning, Stephen. *The Springboard: How Storytelling Ignites Action in Knowledge–Era Organizations.* Boston: Butterworth–Heinemann, 2001.

Fog, Klaus, Christian Budtz, and Baris Yakaboylu. *Storytelling: Branding in Practice.* New York: Springer, 2005.

Gargiulo, Terrence L. *The Strategic Use of Stories in Organizational Communication and Learning.* Armonk, NY: M.E. Sharpe, 2005.

Gunaratnam, Yasmin and David Oliviere. *Narrative and Stories in Healthcare: Illness, Dying and Bereavement.* New York: Oxford University Press (USA), 2009.

Parkin, Margaret. *Tales for Change: Using Storytelling to Develop People and Organizations.* London: Kogan Page, 2004.

Simmons, Annette. *The Story Factor: Inspiration, Influence, and Persuasion Through the Art of Storytelling.* 2nd edition. New York: Basic Books, 2006.

Community Arts Practice

Goldbard, Arlene. *New Creative Community: The Art of Cultural Development..* Oakland, CA: New Village Press, 2006.

Graves, James Bau. Cultural Democracy: The Arts, Community, and the Public Purpose. Champaign, IL: University of Illinois Press, 2004.

Goodman, Steven and Maxine Greene. T*eaching Youth Media: A Critical Guide to Literacy, Video Production, & Social Change.* New York: Teachers College Press, 2003.

Howley, Kevin. Community Media: People, Places, and Communication Technologies. Cambridge, UK: Cambridge University Press, 2005.

Krensky, Beth. *Engaging Classrooms and Communities through Art: A Guide to Designing and Implementing Community-Based Art Education.* Lanham, MD: AltaMira Press, 2008.

Schwarzman, Mat and Keith Knight. *Beginner's Guide to Community-Based Arts.* Oakland, CA: New Village Press, 2005.

General

Birkerts, Sven. *The Gutenberg Elegies: The Fate of Reading in an Electronic Age.* New York: Ballantine, 1994.

Campbell, Joseph. *The Power of Myth.* New York: Doubleday, 1988.

Gilster, Paul. *Digital Literacy.* New York: John Wiley and Sons, Inc., 1997.

McLuhan, Marshall. *Understanding Media: The Extensions of Man.* Cambridge, MA: MIT Press, 1994.

Index

The cover of this book was designed and produced by Rob Kershaw in Adobe Photoshop CS3, using the Chaparral Pro, Stone Sans and Arial Narrow fonts. The cover photograph was taken by Rob Kershaw. The photograph on the back cover was taken by Emily Paulos. The interior of the 3rd edition of this book was reformatted by Oriana Magnera in Myriad Pro and Cambria fonts and was produced in Adobe Indesign CS4.